THE PILGRIMAGE
OF HENRY JAMES

THE PILGRIMAGE
OF HENRY JAMES

BY

VAN WYCK BROOKS

1972

OCTAGON BOOKS

New York

Reprinted 1972
by special arrangement with E. P. Dutton & Co., Inc.

OCTAGON BOOKS
A DIVISION OF FARRAR, STRAUS & GIROUX, INC.
19 Union Square West
New York, N. Y. 10003

PS
2123
B7
1972

LIBRARY OF CONGRESS CATALOG CARD NUMBER: 75-159169

ISBN 0-374-91004-9

Printed in U.S.A. by
NOBLE OFFSET PRINTERS, INC.
NEW YORK 3, N. Y.

NOTE

Readers who are familiar with Henry James will observe that many phrases and even longer passages from his writings have been incorporated in the text of this book, usually without any indication of their source. The author has resorted to this expedient because he knows of no other means of conveying with strict accuracy at moments what he conceives to have been James's thoughts and feelings.

CONTENTS

THE PILGRIMAGE
OF HENRY JAMES

THE PILGRIMAGE OF HENRY JAMES

CHAPTER I

A SMALL BOY AND OTHERS

ON a certain morning in the year 1849, the philosopher Emerson received from a peripatetic friend a letter containing these oddly heretical words: "Considering with much pity our four stout boys, who have no playroom within doors and import shocking bad manners from the street, we gravely ponder whether it wouldn't be better to go abroad for a few years with them, allowing them to absorb French and German, and get such a sensuous education as they cannot get here." Heretical I say these words were, more truly heretical in a sense than any of Emerson's own, for they seemed to contradict the assumptions of the American religion of democracy. One asks oneself what Emerson must have thought as he read them. Perhaps it crossed his mind that if, to a fellow-American, a fellow-philosopher, the out-of-door world had ceased to be a school of manners and a "sensuous education" had become the chief desideratum for one's offspring, it must mean that the

first phase of the great American experiment was
approaching its end.

The letter could not have been written by a New
Englander—its savor was too worldly. Besides, the
New England out-of-doors had still its old bucolic innocence: even in Boston, the Boston of 1849, the "street"
could have given the fond parent little cause for alarm.
And what New Englander of the heroic age would have
desired for his sons an education primarily sensuous?
In fact, the writer, philosopher that he was notwith-
standing, lived, or rather lodged, in New York: he had
in his veins no drop of New England blood and had
never set foot in New England till he was nearly thirty-
five years old. This singular heretic—it was Henry
James the Elder—was of Irish descent on both sides.
Moreover, and as if to seal the disparity between himself
and the illuminati of Boston, the comrades of his youth
had included at least one actor, and there was a family
legend that he had been for a period "quite definitely
wild."

This letter, or rather the purpose which it expressed,
was to have its consequences in American history, for
the William as well as the Henry James of the succeed-
ing generation was largely a product of that sensuous
education in the Old World. On the other hand, both
were largely products of their father. If the elder
James had not possessed the peculiar temperament and
interests that set him apart from his contemporaries,
if he had not inherited a considerable fortune, if, finally,
he had not been the victim of an accident in his youth
that had resulted in the amputation of one of his legs,

the philosophy of his elder and the art of his second son would certainly have been quite different. Having lost this leg, he could live conveniently, as his grandson says, "only in towns where smooth footways and ample facilities for transportation were to be had." It was thus predestined that, in an age when the rustic life was the characteristic American life, his children should pass their infancy on the high roads of the great world.

He was, this man, this witty and devoted, this inveterately urban sage, a figure to the highest degree paradoxical. The son of a prosperous Presbyterian merchant in Albany, he had studied for the ministry and remained, though he never took orders, a theologian by vocation. In his youth, while travelling in England—he was suffering at the time from a nervous disorder—he had become acquainted with the writings of Swedenborg. It was a mystical experience, and it had fixed in him the belief, which his elder son seems to have inherited, that a true enlargement of the spirit is possible only to those who have known sickness, to which he added ostracism and opposition. It was then that he dedicated himself to the formulation of a theology that should express his profound and multiple intuitions. "He applied himself," wrote one of his sons, "with a regularity and a piety as little subject to sighing abatements or betrayed fears as if he had been working under pressure for his bread and ours and the question were too urgent for his daring to doubt." And this although his books, published at his own expense, were received from first to last in "blank silence."

No one but his elder son, who edited his Literary

Remains, has attempted to elucidate what in his own family were known as "Father's Ideas." To us, at least, they must remain flights of the alone to the alone; yet William James expressed what all must feel when he said that his father's style, "to its great dignity of cadence and full and homely vocabulary, united a sort of inward palpitating human quality, gracious and tender, precise, fierce, scornful, humorous by turns, recalling the rich vascular temperament of the old English masters, rather than that of an American of today." The style, in fact, suggests the complexity of the man. Theologian that he was, he had no more sympathy with the moralistic than with the commercial preoccupations of the majority of his countrymen: he had never been able to forget the rigors of his Albany childhood. He delighted in giving the Sabbath a "black eye"; his greatest horror was what he called "flagrant morality," and he said that he would rather have a son of his "corroded with all the sins of the Decalogue than have him perfect." From which we can see that he was in full rebellion against the idols of the tribe.

This singular man was, therefore, in a somewhat trying position. Had he been born a New Englander, had he been shaped by the influences of New England, he might well have become a sort of supplementary Emerson or Thoreau; he might have been able to participate, that is, in the intellectual movement of his age. In this case he would undoubtedly have been reconciled to an American destiny. "An expansive, expanding companion," as Emerson called him, who "would remove to Boston to attend a good club a single night," he was framed for society as others are framed for solitude and would certainly have been a happier man if his social and his intellectual interests had been able to run side by side. In the end he retired to Boston, he settled in Cambridge, he became an ornament of the Saturday Club; and New York knew him no more. As a mystical democrat, a constitutional optimist, a Fourierist of a sort—overflowing, as one of his sons remarks, with a "brave contradiction or opposition between all his parts, a thing which made for perfect variety"—he had indeed much in common with the Transcendentalist brotherhood. Much, but not enough. He could observe that "once we get rid of slavery the new heavens and new earth will swim into reality"; but there he stopped. The truth is that his material resources, his knowledge of the world, his metropolitan view of life had bred in him, along with his theological preoccupations, a sceptical and mundane habit of mind. He had been "wild" and had not repented; he had been the friend of an actor and had not regretted it. New York, in a word, for all its flimsiness and its commerciality, had spoiled him for a more provincial atmosphere: New York was not intellectual, but it was, after all, an outpost of the great world. His elder son speaks of the reckless humor of his conversation and of his "abasing mood" as having "often startled the good people of Boston." He could not take New England seriously.

It was unfortunate. Had anything so irregular, indeed, ever been seen before? This eccentric American was at once too Bostonian for New York and too much of a New Yorker for Boston: he was, moreover, a born controversialist, he loved an argument, he battened on opposition—and where had he been able to find an adversary? In a day of rampant isms, not a soul had listened to *his* particular gospel; he had toiled away in the most awkward of solitudes, and it was not sympathy that he longed for, it was resistance. Resistance! If only the blank wall had returned an echo! If only the blank wall had been *firm!* He had gifts, powers, potentialities: how could he ever discover *what* he had? But America had spoken no word, and he had pushed at the blank wall and found that it was soft; and the bewildered sage, wondering and aggrieved, asked himself whether in Europe his case might not have been different. For Europe he had, on other accounts, a sufficient affection: he loved the color and the romance of life, music, pictures, the past, the ways of the world. Who could tell? Perhaps Europe, which contained everything, might even provide him with a forum. England, for instance. It was in England that he had received the revelation of Swedenborg; he had even formed there in his youth an acquaintance with Carlyle. Possibly, if he returned, he might, in that livelier air, find himself not only welcomed, but embraced, not only embraced, but called out: there were antagonists in England who were worthy of his wit. . . . Such were the fond hopes that possessed him.

The pathos of it was that our anxious philosopher could not, for all his longings, rejoin the European procession. If, in the New World, he dreamed of the Old, he no sooner set foot in Europe than all his American predilections rose up in him. He was the victim of a species of atavism that is common in the younger countries when men, relieved from material pressure, become aware of ancestral instincts that have retained the stamp of their original environment. But the intervening generations had stamped him also: he was American, incorrigibly American, American for good and all. From England he writes home that all the men he meets are "despoiled of their rich individual manliness by the necessity of providing for these imbecile old inheritances of Church and State." "I shouldn't wonder," he observes, "if Barnum grew regenerate in some far-off day by mere force of his democracy." And as for the intellectual life which he had so idealized—alas, how could he have so befooled himself! There was Carlyle, for instance, "Mother Eve's own darling cantankerous Thomas," the greatest man of them all, Carlyle, with his "rococo airs and affectations, his antiquated strut and heroics": Carlyle was simply a "literary desperado." . . . In short, our wistful pilgrim was utterly disabused, disabused and piqued; for it is also true that as a seeker of the English felicity he had experienced, as the younger Henry James remarks, nothing but "the sense of playing his mature and ardent thought over great dense constituted presences and opaque surfaces that could by their very nature scarce give back so much as a shudder." . . . It was all impossible. . . . And yet, and yet . . . He could not surrender the beloved vision. He would walk up and down in his room at the hotel, "talking," as William James describes him, "of the superiority of America to these countries after all, and how much better it is we should have done with them."

But the moment he stepped off the ship the illusion seized him once more. The Old World, was it not a paradise, of which, in the end, by some miracle, the gates might open to receive him? . . . Thus he lived with his eye ever turned across the sea.

Such is the figure who drifts in and out of his second son's reminiscences; such was the man whose temperament, impulses, and preoccupations determined so largely the character and condition of the James family. No doubt Henry James had his father's example in mind when, as he remarks in his life of W. W. Story, he "contrasted the luxury of the European 'career' with the mere snatched dignity of the American." A high talent wasting itself upon the desert air: this was the most poignant spectacle that hung before his eyes during the whole of his adolescence. It would all have been so different beyond the Atlantic! Europe was the land where great men came into their own; Europe was indeed the Jerusalem of all delights. Could anything have been more obvious to a little boy? It was an axiom, an axiom by the nature of the case. "Had *all* their talk," the novelist says of his parents, "had *all* their talk for its subject, in my infant ears, that happy time?" —the time of their first visit to England. "Did it deal only with London and Piccadilly and the Green Park?" And again: "I saw my parents homesick, as I conceived, for the ancient order and distressed and inconvenienced by many of the more immediate features of the modern, as the modern pressed about us, and since their theory of our better living was from an early time that we should renew the quest of the ancient on the very first

possibility I simply grew greater in the faith that somehow to manage that would constitute success in life. I
never found myself deterred from this fond view, which
was implied in every question I asked, every answer I
got, and every plan I formed."

Europe! It was as if Henry James had been born
with a nostalgia for that far-away paradise. Was it
not a legend in the family that he had recalled, from a
visit to Paris in his second year, the wondrous aspect of
the Place Vendôme? He was a preternaturally impressionable little creature, and something had excited him:
his retina had retained the image, at once so harmonious
and so imposing, of the beautiful Parisian square, the
great mansions, the soft line of the roofs, the surprising
column, so erect in the bright air. . . . And then there
had been New York, the cozy back-parlor in Fourteenth
Street, the hearth-rug, the glowing fire. . . . Could he
remember a time when he had not been lying there, in
the fading light of the winter dusk, drinking in the
enchantment of those English picture-books? . . . It
was so warm, so intimate, there was nothing to break
the spell. . . . Europe was all about him: in the Italian
landscape just over his head, in the marble bust of the
Bacchante between the windows, in the golden haze of
the vast Prospect of Florence in the front room—he
could see it through the gap in the red curtains. . . .
The picture-books: they were European too. . . . The
stiff glossy covers, the thick smooth pages, the colors,
deep and rich, chocolate-brown, plum color, claret, and
that funny chalky black. They were not colors, they
were tones. . . . And the scenes, English scenes! . . .

The stable-yard, the sleek fat horses, the blustering master, the coachman with his cockade. Master Jacky, home from Eton for his Christmas holidays, the charred stick in his hand, the footman's immaculate calves, the banisters and the chandelier, the charming young sisters with their golden ringlets, their blooming cheeks, the pretty blue sashes over their fresh muslin gowns. The breakfast-room, the rosy fire in the grate, the toast and the eggs on the table, the comfortable old grandfather unfolding his *Times*. And then the holly and the mistletoe, and the foaming ale, and the obsequious grooms, and the buxom nursemaids, and the gallant fox-hunting gentlemen, their crimson coat-tails on the wind, taking a fence, taking a hedge, taking that little green cottage perhaps. Was there anything one couldn't take—in England, in Europe?

Punch came, and the wonder grew; Dickens came, and he had learned to read; Thackeray came, and Europe was more real to him now than his own three brothers. Europe, or was it only England? He had lived, in a way, so long in England. Those drawings of Leech's! And then *Mrs. Perkins's Ball*, and *Pendennis*, and *David Copperfield*—when had he begun to read them, when had he ceased to hear them read? But there was the Continent too: France and Italy. There was Gavarni's Paris, and Toepffer's droll Geneva. And Florence, where the artists lived, and Rome. It was all a world of colors and forms. . . . Was it wrapped in a sort of iridescent mist? . . . But that was the celestial atmosphere. . . . And every spring his parents had been going back: he was to see it face to face! And every spring they had suddenly changed their minds. Frustration, hope, frustration again—it only fanned his desire.

Thus, for the little boy, the very names of places and things in the other world had become "values and secrets and shibboleths." He had lived in England, lived in Europe, in Thackeray's England, in Toepffer's Europe. . . . What other life, indeed, had he ever known?

America? New York? O yes, he had taken all *that* in! He had absorbed it; he had found it delightful, too. There had been Albany, for holidays and the long summer afternoons, Albany and the old garden sloping down to the stable, and the peach trees: Albany somehow had a flavor of peaches. There were the aunts and the uncles, a bewildering company, all so different, and each with a different legend. And the cousins, the pretty, happy, dancing cousins—they were always dancing: vague airs of the perennial German seemed ever to attend their steps. Had he not himself been taken, a mere mite of observation, to one of Kitty Emmet's "grown-up" assemblies? And there were always the other boys, and school. The Wards, for instance, who were so tough and brown and whose pockets bulged with apples and nuts: any one would have known that the Wards were New Englanders. And Simpson, who boasted that his father was a "stevedore"—mysterious eminence! And the theatre—what a world that had been! And Barnum's Museum. And the summer hotels: the wide verandahs, the ladies with their curls and crinolines and their little parasols, and the gentlemen, bewhiskered and grim-lipped or young and rakish and dressed in blazers and white pantaloons. And there were the artists and authors who were always drifting in and out of the house, Mr. Cole, the "American Turner," and Mr. Powers of the "busts," and "Howadji" Curtis, and Mr. Emerson, whose silvery voice he had heard in the dusk of the back-parlor. And there were the other great men whom he had met, outside, in the street, as he walked about with his hand in his father's: Mr. Sumner, the Senator from Massachusetts, who had stopped and spoken to them, and General Winfield Scott, prodigious with the triumphs of the Mexican War, and Mr. Irving, who had told them how Margaret Fuller—Margaret Fuller of the "Boston connection"—had been drowned the day before on the Jersey coast. Had he missed so much as a breath, a vibration of it all?

He had taken it in, he had listened and looked and marvelled. And yet, it was strange, the whole panorama had simply inflamed his desire. New York, America, *his* America had spoken of Europe with a single voice. There was a confused rumble and rumor in the background that referred to something else, to "business," to politics, to the West, to the mountains and the woods, to strange vague villages and towns with Indian names and names out of history books. But of all these things he had heard so little at home; and there had been no *Punch,* no Gavarni, no Thackeray to make them picturesque and comprehensible. . . . There were the other boys, of course, but he had found the other boys so difficult to play with; and besides, he had never been allowed to remain long enough in any one school to make friends with them. . . . And as for the rest, it had been just like "Europe," a Europe plain instead of a Europe colored! There was the castellated villa on Staten Island, where they had spent the summer: had it not been set up there just in order to remind one of what a real castle might be? And those country-houses on the Hudson—how pale they were beside the lithographs in Nash's *Mansions of England in the Olden Time!* But everything in New York had been like that; everything had sent him back to his dreams and his picture-books. The theatre: the plays he had seen, "London Assurance" and "Nicholas Nickleby," were all so many evocations of Drury Lane. And there were the French acrobats at Barnum's, and the "Bavarian Beauties," and the opera, and Patti—Italian to the last echo. And there were his teachers, Count Adam Gurowski, for instance, the Polish refugee, and the "rank" Russian lady, and Mlle. Delavigne, who had given him lessons at home and who had been simply a Gavarni caricature come to life. And the ladies in the summer hotels had always just been going to Paris, and the gentlemen had always just come back. . . . And then the artists and the authors. An American Turner implied the existence of a European one, and Mr. Powers's busts had all been made in Italy, and "Howadji" Curtis's very name savored of everything foreign. Mr. Irving had been so much like an Englishman, and Mr. Emerson's silvery voice had never been the voice of Fourteenth Street. The others? Alas, for the others, alas, for art in New York! Had they haunted the family fireside for any other purpose than to show a little boy how much more illustrious the artists of the Old World could not fail to be?

"I was somehow in Europe, since everything about me had been 'brought over.'" Thus James himself, in later years, summed up the atmosphere of his childhood. He had seen, he had heard, he had touched, he had all but literally tasted, in the land of his birth, nothing that was not a reflection, a reminder of that romantic other land across the ocean. Had America no identity of its own? Was it all simply a noisy chaos, all that lay outside the sphere of the *cousinage?* Was it all just a rain of atoms, a storm of wind and dust? Something lay outside, beyond, behind, *something;* but why had he always been deterred—oh, so gently deterred—from investigating it? He had not been particularly curious about it. Those outside things, the things that were not "somehow" European—the streets were full of them— had struck him as rather ugly. They repelled him, they were difficult, like the boys at school. . . . Still, why had his parents discouraged him from making friends with the other boys? Or had they discouraged him? It was only a breath, a hint. . . . Not that he greatly cared. . . . But then why were they always changing his schools? . . . Were they afraid of America, afraid of New York?

"I read into the whole connection," Henry James continues, "the chill, or at least the indifference, of a foreseen and foredoomed detachment." Why was it? How had it come about? What was at the bottom of it all? Was it only that the bewildered father, per-

petually in search of a happier environment, could not
submit to giving hostages to that little New York world
in which he had ever been so profoundly ill at ease?
For that father himself, adrift as he was, New York
was only a half-way house. He was a prophet without
honor in his own country, a nomad by the nature of
things: how could he permit his children to take root
in the city of the Philistines? If London was impracticable, New York was impossible—that was sufficiently
clear. But another thought weighed upon his paternal
imagination: New York was also dangerous. He had
before him the example of his own brothers who, liberated as they were from the life of business, the only life
for which that primitive society seemed to afford any
provision, had, as we gather, generally come to grief.
"He regaled us with no scandals," Henry James remarks, "yet it somehow rarely failed to come out that
each contemporary on his younger scene, each hero of
each thrilling adventure, had, in spite of brilliant promise and romantic charm, ended badly, as badly as possible." This, in fact, became for his sons a "grim little
generalization," so striking was the evidence that
"scarce aught but disaster could, in that so unformed
and unseasoned society, overtake young men who were
in the least exposed. Not to have been immediately
launched in business of a rigorous sort," Henry James
continues, "was to *be* exposed, in the absence I mean of
some fairly abnormal predisposition to virtue; since it
was a world so simply constituted that whatever wasn't
business, or exactly an office or a 'store,' places in which
people sat close and made money, was just simply pleas-

ure, sought and sought only in places in which people got tipsy." And moreover, "it was just the ready, even when the moderate, possession of gold that determined, that hurried on, disaster." . . . Such were the fears the benevolent father nursed in his heart. His own brothers, with gold in their pockets, had gone to perdition; and here were his four little boys, eager, imaginative, impressionable—heaven be thanked!—but not cut out for business, and destined in their turn to inherit a share of the Albany gold. How could one be too careful?

It was a little tragicomedy of the New York of the 'fifties. The elder James could have no continuing city; he did not wish to anchor himself—*that* was perfectly true; but he was even more a parent than a philosopher; he had pondered the case, according to his lights, and he was filled with trepidation over the future of that little brood for whose "spiritual decency" he cared, as Henry James remarks, "unspeakably more than for anything else." Thrown in as he was upon himself, he had so few other active concerns. New York was dangerous, he had no doubt of that; and was it not inevitable that, as he saw only New York, he should have looked askance upon American life in general? . . . What did any one really know about this extraordinary national "experiment," this America into which destiny had cast them all and which they had taken as it were on faith, a country without a precedent and almost without a history, which, after the first great epoch of the Revolution, had fallen more and more into the hands of mountebank politicians and rascally business men, a country that certainly provided one with opportunities for making money, but in which it remained to be seen whether the higher human faculties would be able to survive at all? America was the dark continent! Who had understood it, who had explained it? Could one trust it? Could one go on, like the poets and the statesmen, protesting even the stoutest optimism? . . . How natural it was, in those last dispiriting years before the Civil War, that such thoughts should have invaded the mind of a sensitive fellow-citizen of Mr. Astor the fur-merchant and Commodore Vanderbilt of the Erie! In the South men had their soil, and they lived by the faith of the soil. There was the West: for millions the West was a religion. The New England air still vibrated with the memories of the Revolution; and besides, if New England and the South had retained their colonial sentiment, they were impregnated with the traditions of American statesmanship. New York, on the other hand, was the metropolis, and those who loved the world foregathered there; but its own traditions had been lost and forgotten, trampled away by the ravenous feet of trade. It was the last quarter in which to seek either for the traces of the American past or for the omens of the American future. Natural it was, therefore, that the elder James, reflecting upon his family history, should have asked himself, in his gloomier moments, how far America itself was not responsible for "such a chronicle," as one of his sons describes it, "of early deaths, arrested careers, broken promises, orphaned children." Our sage, in short, our theologian, the father of those four impressionable boys, had become the victim of an obsession. American life was a quicksand in which everything one held most dear was in peril of being engulfed and lost. At all hazards one's own children must be prevented from getting their feet entangled in it.

Thus at the outset Henry James was shielded from any touch of the *profanum vulgus.* "It meanwhile fairly overtakes and arrests me," he writes in his reminiscences, "that our general medium of life in the circumstances I speak of was such as to make a large defensive verandah, which seems to have very stoutly and completely surrounded us, play more or less the part of a raft of rescue in too high a tide, too high a tide there about us of the ugly and the graceless." The ugly and the graceless were, to be sure, nine-tenths of human life; but that was the point, it was life itself this father feared on behalf of his children—since life, for them, presented itself in American terms alone. Endless were to be the consequences of all this in the career of Henry James. Even his brother William was to find it difficult to overcome that inherited fear: he might never have overcome it, in fact, if he had not found in Agassiz a great master to reassure him, to convince him not only that America was "all right," but that it offered him an adequate scope for *his* particular genius. Indeed, how far was not that final "plunge" of William James's, that philosophic, that pragmatic plunge into what he called "the muddy stream of things," an almost conscious reaction against the "tender-mindedness" of the circle of his childhood? For Henry James America was to afford no Agassiz; he was to encounter no parallel case of an artist, a man of letters, eminent, equipped, magnetic, and at the same time at home in the new chaotic generation as Emerson, Prescott, Hawthorne had been at home in the simpler world of the past. In short, he was to find no Virgil for the dark path; and besides, he was more passive than his brother; he could not so easily react; he received impressions and he retained them. Europe was a paradise. America was a wilderness—it signified nothing but calamity, destruction, oblivion.

In time, in the far future, the life and writings of Henry James were to manifest the effects of all these early—shall we call them?—illusions. They grew, they flourished: "brooding monster" that he was, or was to call himself, "born to discriminate *à tout propos*," how many preconceptions were to embed themselves in the depths of his mind, gradually, silently, how much of a sort of preliminary discrimination was to be imposed upon him, as it were, determining the field and the conditions of his fastidious thought! He accepted these idols of the provincial cave that had been bred so naturally by the character, the circumstances, the solicitude of his father, by the situation of his family, and all the influences of his childhood contributed to foster them.

For if he was protected from the common life, to what was he exposed? To the life of that little New York society which, if it was "open wide," as he says, "to the east and comparatively to the south," the east and the south that signified Europe and the lingering European order, was yet "screened in somehow conveniently from north and west." So far as the world of "business" was concerned, "the word had been passed, all round," he remarks, "that we didn't, that we couldn't and shouldn't, understand these things." But when, from that little screened society, the element of business was subtracted, what was left? What was left for a child to absorb, a child so impressionable that "figures, faces, furniture, sounds, smells and colors" had become for him "a positive little orgy of the senses and riot of the mind"? Nothing, virtually, but echoes of the *beau monde* across the ocean. Along with business the men had vanished from the scene: there remained only, as our author remarks in one of his prefaces, "the music-masters and French pastry-cooks, the ladies and children —immensely present and immensely numerous these, but testifying with a collective voice to the extraordinary absence . . . of a single male interest." What remained, in short, was "the wondrous fact that ladies might live for pleasure, pleasure always, pleasure alone." Ah, that New York society of the Age of Innocence, of N. P. Willis and *Nothing to Wear!* Ah, those dreams of the Tuileries, of Paris gowns and English lords! Ask the freshets in the spring why they run to the deep sea!

Henry James looked and listened. What did he hear? What ingenuous and charming discourses on the conduct of life? What hymns to the Graces? What notes of a perpetual song in which the artless and the elegant, the virginal and the voluptuous were blended in equal measure? This little society, so intensely feminine, was it not an unregarded, but ever so keenly regarding protectorate, as it were, of the fashionable world of England and France? How natural it was then that, in the midst of his romantic dream of the Old World, a second romantic dream should have begun to take form in

Henry James's mind. Countesses, duchesses, great
ladies, noble gentlemen were so obviously the heroes and
the heroines of the wondrous European fairy-tale! That
was the New York idea, and all the stories he had read,
all the pictures he had absorbed, had prepared him to
believe it: the great world was a world beyond good
and evil. . . . Was it another illusion, this fruit of a
sequestered adolescence? But what "reality" of his
own had he ever experienced? He had been removed
from the discipline of the streets: had he been subjected to any other discipline? He had "read too many
novels." And his father's "Ideas" had been so impalpable: how could he have derived from *that* source any
interpretation of the universe? The elder James had
been so irrepressibly optimistic; he had had such a
cloudless faith in human nature; he had heard so much
about discipline in his own bitter Presbyterian youth;
he had trusted his children to find the right pasturage
for their souls. . . . But admitting that problem about
the other boys (who were "so difficult to play with"),
admitting that they had "no companions," would a little
history, not to say a little more Latin and Greek, not to
add a little more continuity, have come amiss?

At twelve, Henry James had at last been taken to
Europe; at sixteen he had been brought home again.
His family had abandoned New York; henceforward,
until he was twenty-one, Newport was to remain his
home. But for four years, the years of awakening, he
had experienced in the Old World a riot of "recognitions"; he had been so "pierced," as he put it later,
"by the sharp outland dart, as to be able ever after-

wards but to move about, vaguely and helplessly'' with the shaft still in his side. Ah, that Europe of the complex order and the colored air! There had been the first night in London . . . the thick, heavy smell of the atmosphere that had given him such a sense of possession. There had been the soft summer evening when they had arrived in Paris and he had hung over the balcony, drinking in the shadowy mystery of the rue de la Paix. There had been the old inn at Lyons, so redolent of the true *vie de province* and of all the voices and graces of the past. And the first castle, the first ruin, the first peasant in sabots! There had been the old thick-walled, green-shuttered pension-school at Geneva; and Boulogne, where Thackeray's world had come to life under his eyes; and the legendary woods at Bonn. And London again, Hogarth's London, and Paris, the old and the new. He had seen the Empress, young and fair and shining; he had seen the baby Prince Imperial borne amid glittering swords on his progress to Saint-Cloud. And there had been the Luxembourg and the great still rooms of the Louvre, the left bank, the quays, the old bookshops, the long black rue de Seine. Above all, he had had his taste—such a tantalizing taste!—of the *beau monde* itself. Was he ever to forget that English family at Geneva to whom, in the first flush of their own admiration for *Adam Bede,* his parents had confidingly lent the book? "I catch again," he writes in his reminiscences, "the echo of their consternation on receiving it back with the remark that all attempt at an interest in such people, village carpenters and Methodists, had proved vain—for *that* style of Anglo-Saxon;

together with that of my own excited wonder about such other people, those of the style in question, those somehow prodigiously presented by so rare a delicacy, so proud a taste, and made thus to irradiate a strange historic light." And there had been the pretty young Marquise, "unmistakably 'great,' exhaling from afar," as he had encouraged himself to imagine, "the scented air of the Tuileries," who had looked into their compartment, where her own servants were travelling, on that memorable journey from Cologne to Paris, and smiled, and even pouted, through her elegant patience. She had "caused to swim before me somehow," he says, "such a view of happy privilege at the highest pitch as made me sigh the more sharply, even if the less professedly, for our turning our backs on the complex order, the European." . . . He had, in short, absorbed the European virus; he had come home with an aching prevision of "the comparative, not to say the absolute, absence of tonic accent in the appearances complacently awaiting" him.

He had come home, home to Newport. His affections had been fixed irretrievably upon the Old World. Picturesque Europe, social Europe: ah, that sublime synthesis of his early reveries! Who could question it? Was it not for ever the Great Good Place, the abode of honor, order, beauty, of all the elegances? That was the faith of Newport, at least, old Newport, the Newport of the "mildly and reminiscentially desperate," the Newport of those who were always going back, again, and again, and yet again, "with a charming, smiling, pleading inconsequence," the Newport of the "inverted romantics," of the wanderers between two worlds, the America for which Europe had unfitted them, and the Europe which, Americans as they were, they had never been able to call their own. Newport was not New York, the New York of the music-masters and the French pastry-cooks. The bright, the brisk, the fresh, the artless had, in a measure, given place there to the mellow, the crepuscular, the retrospective. There was a difference, a difference of note, a difference of tone. . . . Morning and evening. . . . But were they not a morning and an evening of the same day? . . . In the one society as in the other the great world across the sea was the dream of every heart. Criticism only began "after that."

It was here, encircled by his family and John La Farge, in that "wondrous esoteric quarter," as he describes it, "peopled just by us and our friend and our common references," that Henry James set to work to learn the craft of a writer. He was already a "novelist *en herbe*"; and he had himself perceived that his impressions "were naught without a backing, a stout stiff hard-grained underside that would hold them together and of which the terrible name was simply science, otherwise learning, and learning exclusively by books." He was to become a novelist, in short, by studying other novelists: such was the design with which he assumed the obligations of an apprenticeship that was to have, in its own way, so marvellous a flowering. The circumstances of his life and character were to intensify, as the years passed, this self-dedication of the craftsman; meanwhile, we observe that his reading confirmed the romantic prepossessions with which he looked out upon the world. Who that has turned the pages of the *Notes of a Son and Brother* can forget the ardor of those references to the *Revue des Deux Mondes?* It took its place, the great review, it took its place, for James at Newport, "as the very headspring of culture, a mainstay in exile, and"—let us note his words—"as opening wide in especial the doors of that fictive portrayal of a society which put a price, for the brooding young reader, on cases, on *cadres,* in the Revue parlance, already constituted and propitiously lighted. Then it was," our author continues, "that the special tension of the dragged-out day from Cologne to Paris proved, on the absurdest scale, a preparation, justified itself as a vivid point of reference: I was to know what the high periodical meant when I encountered in its *études de mœurs* the blue-chinned corruptible, not to say corrupt, *larbin* and the smart *soubrette;* it was, above all, a blessing to feel myself, in the perusal of M. Octave Feuillet, an education, as I supposed, of the taste, not at a marked disadvantage; since who but the Petite Comtesse herself had swung her crinoline in and out of my prospect, or, to put it better, of my preserved past, on one of my occasions of acutest receptivity?" . . . Ah, yes, M. Octave Feuillet, and Balzac, for that matter, Balzac, whom he had read—all of him—as a school-boy! *The great world was the great theme of the great novelists:* had not some such principle as this already begun to take form in James's mind? . . . If one meant to be a great novelist—one must—somehow—the great world.— But how?—Where?—In America?—That was a little perplexing.—But one could leave so much to the future.

He had passed into a silent ecstasy of dreams, thoughts, plans. "The above-mentioned H.," his brother William writes in a letter of the time, "could in no wise satisfy my craving for knowledge of family and friends —he didn't seem to have been on speaking terms with anyone for some time past, and could tell me nothing of what they did, said or thought, about any given subject." He was immersed in his own fantasies—"not a little mildly—though oh *so* mildly—morose or anxiously mute," as he remembered later; he felt within himself the stir of a prodigious talent. And thus, confined within that warm little coterie, circumfused with the air of his father's household, an air "stimulating," as a visitor described it, "like that of a high mountain near the tropics," he began to premeditate the creation of a world of his own. He had reached, let us add in his own words, the age of twenty "in well-nigh grotesque unawareness of the properties of the atmosphere in which he but wanted to claim that he had been nourished."

CHAPTER II

IN the last story that he published, *The Jolly Corner*, James presents an expatriate like himself, Spencer Brydon, who, returning to New York after an absence of a quarter of a century, finds himself obsessed with thoughts of what his destiny might have been if he had remained in America. He still owns the old house on lower Fifth Avenue, the "jolly corner" in which he had passed his childhood: it is empty and deserted and full of dusty memories, and Brydon falls into the habit of passing his nights there, roaming through the great blank chambers and evoking the past. "It's only a question," he says to a friend, "of what fantastic, yet perfectly possible, development of my own nature I may not have missed. It comes over me that I had then a strange *alter ego* deep down somewhere within me as the full-blown flower is in the small tight bud, and that I just took the course, just transferred him to the climate, that blighted him at once and forever." And thereupon he becomes convinced that the old house is still haunted by the self who stayed at home. Who is he, what is he, what has he become, that abandoned, that American self? Brydon, invaded by the illusion, stalks

27

the ghost; and at last, one night, in the first glimmering
of the dawn, he becomes aware that it has actually taken
form.   Prowling about the house, he has himself opened
a certain door; he returns to the room and finds it closed.
Shall he open it?   It comes over him that the other
Brydon does not wish to be seen.   He hesitates; he
masters his curiosity; he turns away; he has decided not
to pursue the reluctant spirit.   He descends the stairs;
then he perceives that the street door stands open.   The
figure is before him, against the wall, with its hands over
its face.   Brydon starts forward; the hands drop; it is
a face of horror.   And Brydon faints and falls upon
the floor.

It is impossible to mistake the personal bearing of this
story, impossible to question the implication of that
face of horror which presents itself to Brydon.   Who
can doubt that it expresses a conviction which James
himself had never outlived, a conviction that, but for
the grace of Europe, his life too would have ended in
some monstrous fiasco?   His return to America at seven-
teen, after his first long visit to the Old World, had
signified, to his aching fancy, as he tells us, "premature
abdication, sacrifice and, in one dreadful word, failure."
How did he feel in his old age?   "When I think," he
wrote to Mrs. William James in 1913, "when I think of
how little Boston and Cambridge were of old ever *my*
affair, or anything but an accident, for me, of the
parental life there to which I occasionally and painfully
and losingly sacrificed, I have a superstitious terror of
seeing them at the end of time again stretch out strange
inevitable tentacles to draw me back and destroy me."

A superstitious terror! Strange inevitable tentacles! James was a man of seventy when he wrote that.

To the end of his life, then, and however disenchanting his experience of Europe may have been, America, to James, signified failure and destruction. It was the dark country, the sinister country, where the earth was a quicksand, where amiable uncles ended in disaster, where men were turned into machines, where genius was subject to all sorts of inscrutable catastrophes. He had taken to heart numberless examples that seemed to have been placed, as if to warn him, directly in his path. There was his father, whose mind he had never understood, but whose brilliant capacity was no more obvious than the fact that somehow he had mysteriously failed to effectuate himself. There was William Page, the painter, the friend of the family, whose extraordinary pictures were already turning black and vanishing from their canvases owing to "some fallacy as to pigments, some perversity as to basis, too fondly, too blindly entertained," as James was to remark later, a tragic story of waste, of "unlighted freedom of experiment possible only (for it comes back to that) in provincial conditions." There was Washington Allston, whose talent had grown thinner and vaguer every day in the bleak atmosphere of Cambridgeport: long and long James had looked at that last unfinished, labored canvas of his in the Boston Athenæum, drinking in the lesson that he was constrained to draw from it. The American artist in the American air was a doomed man: pitfalls surrounded him on every side. Was not even Hawthorne a case in point, Hawthorne who had himself attributed the paucity of his productions to a "total lack of sympathy at the age when his mind would naturally have been most effervescent"? What might not Hawthorne have become if he had sprung from another soil! . . . Thus Henry James read his own fears into the world that surrounded him. Was there any occasion for these fears, any justification in the facts of the case itself? It suffices to say that he felt them: the instances to which I have referred, and which are all to be found in his writings, show us how constantly his mind was occupied with this question. We remember how the narrator in *The Aspern Papers* marvels that Jeffrey Aspern, that American Shelley of the previous age, had "found means to live and write like one of the first; to be free and general and not at all afraid; to feel, understand and express everything." We remember the moral that James tells us he had drawn from Hawthorne's case before his first naïve opinion of Hawthorne had been subjected to the test of his friend H. B. Brewster's "cosmopolitan culture," the moral "that an American could be an artist, one of the finest, without 'going outside' about it." Clearly, Hawthorne to James's mind was the exception that proved the rule, the rule that, without "going outside," an American could not be an artist at all, and even Hawthorne ceased to be an entirely convincing exception. As for Poe, Thoreau, Whitman, whose poems he was so soon to read, they could never have dispelled his apprehensions. Of Poe he said, that "to take him with more than a certain degree of seriousness is to lack seriousness oneself"; and of Thoreau, that "he is worse than provincial, he is

parochial." And he accused Whitman of "discharging
the undigested contents of his blotting-book into the lap
of the public." It might be said of these estimates that
they reveal simply a series of legitimate personal antipathies, though I think they suggest more than a little
of that provincial humility, that inability to believe that
any good thing could come out of the American
Nazareth, which he exhibited when he found his opinion
of Hawthorne so sadly reduced at the approach of a
Europeanized friend. My present point, however, is
that, feeling as he did about the greatest of his prede-
cessors, he could find neither in the world about him nor
in the history and traditions of that world anything to
reassure him, anything to counterbalance the fears, the
dread, with which from the first he had looked out upon
it. The "striking evidence" of his childhood that
"scarce aught but disaster *could,* in that so unformed
and unseasoned society, overtake young men who were
in the least exposed" was confirmed for him now in the
artistic as well as in the general human sphere: "exposure," he was evidently convinced, signified disaster
as much for the American artist as for the American
young man. He could not, in the phrase of one of his
contemporaries, keep himself too carefully in cotton.

Such were the prepossessions with which, at the outset
of his career, Henry James appears to have regarded the
American scene. Was he not, for comprehensible reasons, the prey of that "fear of life" to which Flaubert
also confessed himself a victim? Undoubtedly; and to
this may be traced perhaps the deep longing for security,
privacy, ceremony that was to mark his later years. But

to return from the ultimate to the immediate, what a light this fact seems to throw upon the great "renunciation" with which his career opened! In the *Notes of a Son and Brother* he describes a certain moment when, as he was sailing back to Newport one evening after a visit to a camp of wounded soldiers at Portsmouth Grove, a sudden "realization" had come to him, a "strange rapture" of realization, that one might be "no less exaltedly than wastefully engaged in the common fact of endurance." He means that the passive *rôle*, the *rôle* of the spectator of life, had suddenly been endowed in his eyes with a certain high legitimacy: he who had been prevented by an accident from taking part in the Civil War had "worked out," as Miss Rebecca West puts it, "a scheme of existence . . . in which the one who stood aside and felt rather than acted acquired thereby a mystic value, a spiritual supremacy, which—but this was perhaps a later development of the theory—would be rubbed off by participation in action." In this faith, as we know, James was to live ever after. But would he have embraced it with such a "strange rapture" if, for him, life, action, passion had not been invested with singular terrors?

It is with some such question as this in our minds that we see him emerging from the New England of the 'sixties. His family had left Newport; they had settled in Cambridge. Not till he was twenty-seven was Henry James to return to Europe for a second visit. Meanwhile, upon what sort of scene was he destined to look out? In what light does he himself appear to us? What thoughts filled his mind? We seem to see a grave and somewhat priestlike figure, sedate and watchful, guarded in his movements, slow and hesitating in speech. He has not yet acquired that look of an Elizabethan sea-captain that is to accompany the black, silky beard of his early London days; he suggests rather some Hellenized Roman of the third century, though there are times when his personality is enveloped in a kind of shadow. He is reserved and yet, one would say, eager for experience, affectionate and suspicious, precise and slightly prosaic, but full of the keenest sort of aesthetic subtleties. His talk, enchanting in the presence of a single companion, bristles with intense little preferences and sharp little exclusions. His personal pride appears to be almost morbidly over-developed. Of what is he thinking? He has not been able to forget the humiliation of those first hours of the war, his accident, his invalidism. He remembers his childhood, the failure that he had been in the eyes of his tutors, his inability either to grasp the rudiments of his studies or to play with other boys. He had scarcely known a time in those days when he would not have been willing to exchange his lot for that of somebody else, with the assured certainty of gaining by the bargain! He is determined to vindicate his existence, to write as man has never written before: has he not convinced himself, in the face of Mr. Lincoln's call for volunteers, that this might be "at least a negative of combat, an organized, not a loose and empty one, something definitely and firmly parallel to action in the tented field"? He is infinitely curious about life; his sensibilities are clear and fresh. For the rest, he is circumspect and somewhat prim. Should an artist have passions? He believes that an examination of this question is always premature. Like Longmere, in *Madame de Mauves*, he has in his composition a lurking principle of asceticism to whose authority he has ever paid an unquestioning respect. Like Longueville, in *Confidence*, he is annoyed when he discovers that he has obeyed a force which he was unable to measure at the time; he has little taste for giving himself up and never does so without very soon wishing to take himself back. Like Roderick Hudson, in the latter's first phase, he has a tendency to regard all things in the light of his art, to hand over his impulses to his genius to be dealt with, to invest every gain of soul or sense in the enterprise of planned production. For the rest, if he has been estranged from life, his lot has been cast amid conditions that are the least calculated to win him back again. . . . "The generation between 1865 and 1895," as Henry Adams remarks, "was already mortgaged, and no one knew it better than the generation itself." . . . Henry James knows it, knows it in advance: has he failed to catch the signs of the times, to foresee the chaos of the new age, the decline of the social life of his countrymen, the drop of the American barometer? Far from reassuring is the spectacle that lies before him. The age of faith has come to an end; the age of business has begun.

One pictures Henry James, then, peering anxiously into the future, terrified by countless omens of a wrath to come. . . . He saw himself confronted with a population given over comprehensively to what Mr. Rockefeller was to describe as sawing wood; for such as himself, he must have felt, there was as little room in

his own country as there was for Alice at the Mad
Hatter's table. "She found her chief happiness," our
author says of the repatriated American baroness in
The Europeans, "in the sense of exerting a certain
power and making a certain impression; and now she
felt the annoyance of a rather wearied swimmer who,
on nearing shore, to land, finds a smooth straight wall
of rock where she had counted upon a clean firm beach.
Her power, in the American air, seemed to have lost its
prehensible attributes; the smooth wall of rock was in-
surmountable." So it seemed to James, no doubt; he had
no single point of contact with what a contemporary
was to describe as this new "bankers' Olympus." Nor
was Boston capable of arousing his affection. Those
years in the New England capital were marked, to quote
Henry Adams again, by "a steady decline of literary
and artistic intensity. . . . Society no longer seemed
sincerely to believe in itself or anything else." We have
it all, or much of it, in *The Bostonians*, that admirable
novel which deserves its generic title; we have there a
most memorable image of the aftermath of the heroic
age, the ebb-tide of all those humanitarian impulses
which, at an exceptional hour and at the hands of exceptional men, had assumed such elevated if rather
fantastic forms, and had now lost themselves in fatuity
and petrifaction. To James, who had no hereditary
associations with it, whose mind reverberated with the
echoes of the great world, and who saw it now in its
hour of *Götterdämmerung*, Boston was nothing if not
repellent: he expressed the feeling of a lifetime when he
placed in the mouth of Christopher Newman the opinion

that those who spoke ill of the United States should be carried home in irons and compelled to live in the neighborhood of the Back Bay. "What it all came to saying," as he remarks in his life of W. W. Story, apropos of the latter's attempt to adjust himself to an earlier Boston, "was that, with an alienated mind, he found himself again steeped in a society both fundamentally and superficially *bourgeois,* the very type and model of such a society, presenting it in the most favorable, in the most admirable light; so that its very virtues irritated him, so that its ability to be strenuous without passion, its cultivation of its serenity, its presentation of a surface on which it would appear to him that the only ruffle was an occasionally acuter spasm of the moral sense, must have acted as a tacit reproach." And Story had "belonged"; and that had been Boston at its best!

Boston! And, beyond Boston, that great unendowed, unfurnished, unentertained, and unentertaining continent where one sniffed as it were the very earth of one's foundations! "I shall freeze after this sun," said Albrecht Dürer, as he turned homeward across the Alps from Italy. And where was James to turn for warmth, he whose every fibre longed for that other gracious world, that soft, harmonious, picturesque "Europe" of his imagination, that paradise of form, color, style from which he had been ravished away and which had captured and retained, as in some delirious, some alas, too soon interrupted embrace, the virtue, the very principle of his desire, his fancy, his every in-

stinct? Ah, that secret passionate ache, that rebellious
craving of the unsatisfied senses! One felt like a travel-
ler in the desert, deprived of water and subject to the
terrible mirage, the torment of illusion, of the thirst-
fever. One heard the plash of fountains, one saw the
green gardens, the orchards, hundreds of miles away.
Europe. And then this emptiness, this implacable emptiness: not a shadow, nothing but the glare of a commonplace prosperity. . . . There were moments, to be
sure, when Boston seemed almost European. How one
rejoiced in those quiet squares, in the ruddy glow of the
old brick walls in the late October sunlight! And there
was Norton's great brown study at Shady Hill. . . .
But one seemed somehow to lose the feeling of one's
identity, one seemed to breathe in a vacuum. There
was so little spontaneity in the air; it was all so earnest,
or so cold and restrained, or so complacent—wit itself
in Boston seemed to be a function of complacency. And
outside, in the streets, how shrill were the voices, how
angular were the gestures, how deficient somehow in
weight, volume, and resonance were the souls one discerned in these hurrying passers-by! . . . And there
was the Cambridge horse-car, clattering along through
the dust on its lazy everlasting way: one could sit there
on a summer noon, utterly alone, jogging home to one's
work-table, with a sense of being on the periphery of
the universe, twenty thousand leagues from the nearest
centre of energy. One stared through the dingy pane
of the window at the bald, bare, bleak panorama that
seemed to shuffle past: an unkempt field, and then a

wooden cottage, and then another wooden cottage, a rough front yard, a little naked piazza, a footway over-laid with a strip of planks.

Was it all like this, was it all a void or a terror? He had received every encouragement, certainly; and yet he had never been really drawn out, as young men were drawn out—or weren't they?—in England, in France. People seemed somehow never to expect one to become, or even to want one to become, what one was determined to become. A portent, a veritable genius—that would have been so disconcerting in Boston! There was something a little indecent in the mere thought of such a thing: it appeared to be taken for granted that a bright young American ought not to make himself too conspicuous, ought not even to desire a destiny that deviated too far from the common lot. And then there were those prescriptions, those impalpable moulds that one was supposed to have accepted. There was Howells's repeated warning, for instance, against not "ending happily": one labored always under the conviction that to terminate a fond æsthetic effort in felicity had to be as much one's obeyed law as to begin it and carry it on in the same rosy mood. And in any case—granting that one didn't, for one's life, for the very life of one's imagination, dare to penetrate too far beyond one's own circle—how could one ever create a *comédie humaine* out of the world at one's disposal? It was utterly, fantastically impossible!

Years later, in London, Henry James told his friend Mr. E. S. Nadal that before deciding to live in Europe he had given his own country a "good trial." It was true;

for the greater part of a decade he kept his eyes fixed upon the American scene, and even then for a number of years he seems not to have relinquished the idea of returning to it. "I know what I am about," he writes at thirty-five to William James, "and I have always my eyes on my native land." But there was something that came between him and the picture, something that is revealed in the fact that he endeavored to find America in such places as Newport and Saratoga: a certain pattern that he had drawn from his reading had taken shape in his imagination, and he could look in the world about him only for the traces of that alien literary world. He could scarcely conceive indeed of an art of fiction that dispensed with the *mise-en-scène* of the writers he admired. Was this merely, was it purely, a matter of spontaneous taste? Is it not more accurate to say that a certain preconception had taken root at the very base of his literary consciousness? By whatever name we are to call the vision that filled his mind, he expressed it, in any case, in the following passage in his life of Hawthorne—a passage that explains better than anything else the rift between himself and his own country:

It takes so many things, as Hawthorne must have felt later in life, when he made the acquaintance of the denser, richer, warmer European spectacle—it takes such an accumulation of history and custom, such a complexity of manners and types, to form a fund of suggestion for a novelist. . . . The negative side of the spectacle on which Hawthorne looked out, in his contemplative saunterings and reveries, might, indeed, with a little ingenuity, be made almost ludicrous; one might enumerate the items of high civilization, as it exists in other countries, which are absent from the texture of American life, until it should become a wonder to know what was left. No State, in the European sense of the word, and indeed barely a specific national name. No sovereign, no court, no personal loyalty, no aristocracy, no church, no clergy, no army, no diplomatic service, no country gentlemen, no palaces, no castles, nor manors, nor old country-houses, nor parsonages, nor thatched cottages, nor ivied ruins; no cathedrals, nor abbeys, nor little Norman churches, nor great universities, nor public schools— no Oxford, nor Eton, nor Harrow; no literature, no novels, no museums, no pictures, no political society, no sporting class—nor Epsom nor Ascot! Some such list as that might be drawn up of the absent things in American life—especially in the American life of forty years ago, the effect of which, upon an English or a French imagination, would probably, as a general thing, be appalling. The natural remark, in the almost lurid light of such an indictment, would be that if these things are left out, everything is left out. The American knows that a good deal remains; what it is that remains— that is his secret, his joke, as one may say.

It could not have occurred to James in the 'seventies that most of the items he enumerates here are absent as much from the texture of Russian and Scandinavian as from that of American life—which was not to prevent the emergence in Russia and Scandinavia of a fiction entirely comparable with that of England and France. The evidence for such a deduction was still to come, at least for an American reader; but so much for the general law involved in this bill of the novelist's rights. Was Howells mistaken when, in his review of James's book, he remarked that after one had omitted all these paraphernalia one had "simply the whole of human life left"? Was there anything, anything but the limitations—the mental configuration, rather—of the individual himself, to make it impossible for an artist to shape in prose the material that Whitman, for example, had found so abundantly at hand? However this may be, James had taken his world and his scale of values from the fiction with which his mind was saturated. He was thus destined to make certain exactions of America which America could not fulfil.

For if it was a question of palaces, castles, thatched cottages, and ivied ruins, if it was a question of the "luxuries and splendors of life," of "ambassadors, ambassadorial compliments, Old World drawing-rooms, with duskily moulded ceilings," if it was a question of such things as these, of which, like the hero of *Watch and Ward*, James himself "liked to be reminded," then America was unprofitable indeed. There was the New York of the dancing-masters—a world of echoes. There was Boston society, but that was a "boy and girl institution," a "Sammy and Billy, a Sallie and Millie affair," as another caustic observer had just remarked, "very pleasant and jolly for young people, but, so far as the world and its ways were concerned, little more than a big village development." And between the two there was Mrs. Howe, propounding, alas, apropos of the new-born son of her Newport neighbor, the Turkish minister Blaque Bey, the riddle, Can a baby a Bey be? "Mrs. Howe was very gay," writes Colonel Higginson in his diary, "and sang her saucy song of 'O So-ci-e-ty,' which is so irreverent to Beacon Street that I wondered how the A's could remain in the field.'' Henry James, with his inner eye fixed upon the denser, richer, warmer European spectacle that filled his imagination, upon the palaces, the castles, that had formed such a fund of suggestion for the novelists he revered—Henry James might easily have listened to that saucy song, and with what a sinking of the heart. Clearly, as he was to put it later, the apple of America was not to be negotiated by any such teeth as his.

Later on, after he had settled in London and could look back upon these years of indecision, he was to find that certain aspects of American life had left upon his mind indelible impressions. He was then to produce, in *Washington Square* and *The Bostonians,* the most brilliant pictures of the two cities in which he had lived: the New York that he had absorbed as a child and the Boston that he had observed in the heightened light of the war. He had known his America, he had understood it, far more deeply than he had ever supposed. Moreover, it had formed his instincts, his vital standards, stamped him for good and all; and it had given him, along with so much that was bitter, his one love, the love that was still to throb, like a dying pulse, in the last sentient creature, a woman among ghosts, of his later art. Yes, America was his world, bone of his bone, the world of his essential self; and yet as long as he was in that world he could see it, as Don Quixote saw Spain, only in terms of the novels that possessed his imagination. As a boy, he had written a letter to an actress in Boston who had sent him in return a printed copy of her play, ''addressed,'' as he

says, "in a hand which assumed a romantic cast as soon
as I had bethought myself of finding for it a happy
precedent in Pendennis's Miss Fotheringay." He had
never ceased to read into the incidents of his life, into
the scenes that confronted him, associations with the
novelized Europe from which he had drawn such "mystic strength": he had caught in the legend of his
father's friendship with Edwin Forrest echoes of the
diaries and memoirs of "the giftedly idle and the fash-
ionably great, the Byrons, the Bulwers, the Pelhams,
the Coningsbys"; he had seen in Miss Upham's board-
ing-house in Cambridge a translation in American terms
of Balzac's Maison Vauquer; he had found in his cousin
Robert Temple, newly returned from Europe, a character "in the sense," as he puts it, "in which 'people
in books' were characters, and other people, roundabout
us, were somehow not. . . . We owed him to Dickens
or Thackeray, the creators of superior life to whom we
were at that time always owing most." And as the
years had gone by and the American scene had failed
to stimulate his interest on its own account, he had
continued to romanticize it in this way, re-creating it in
the image of the pattern within his brain. Glance at
his stories of this period. In *Crawford's Consistency*,
Elizabeth is brought up "in the manner of an Italian
princess of the Middle Ages," in a "high-hedged old
garden" at Orange, New Jersey. In *De Grey: A Romance*, Mrs. De Grey keeps a priest in her house to
serve as her confessor. In *Poor Richard*, the young New
England farmer is represented as kissing Gertrude's
hand whenever he meets her, while she, a homespun

Yankee by every implication of her being, maintains in her rustic parlor the ritual of an English country-house. In *Eugene Pickering*, the story turns upon the fact that a marriage had been arranged when Eugene was a boy between himself and the daughter of one of his father's friends. "I have an especial fondness for going into churches on week-days," says Miss Guest, in *Guest's Confession*. "One does it in Europe, you know; and it reminds me of Europe." Virtually all these early stories of James's are the fruit of a similar nostalgia, a similar effort to discover in the American world the traces of a Europe either of memory or of fantasy: their creator was as much out of key with the scene upon which his eyes rested as Roger Lawrence, in *Watch and Ward*, standing on the piazza of his house and surveying the bursting spring through an opera-glass. As for the American spectacle in and of itself, he could make nothing of it. "I believe I should be a good patriot," says Miss Condit, in *The Impressions of a Cousin*, "if I could sketch my native town. But I can't make a picture of the brown-stone stoops in the Fifth Avenue, or the platform of the elevated railway in the Sixth. . . . I can sketch the palazzo and can do nothing with the uptown residence." And this was precisely the situation of Henry James.

In his old age, when he returned to America, he commented on "the thinness, making too much for transparency, for the effect of paucity, still inherent in American groupings; a law under which the attempt to subject them to portraiture, to see them as 'composing,' resembles the attempt to play whist with an imperfect pack of cards.'' Well he remembered that sensation of helplessness, of impotence, as of those creatures of the deep sea who change color and shrink when they are astray in fresh water. He had felt so baffled, so powerless in this environment that refused to conform to the shapes within his brain; he had not been able to conquer his world, and every day it had seemed to him more menacing. ''Long would it take,'' he says in his reminiscences, ''to tell why [New England] figured as a danger, and why that impression was during the several following years much more to gain than to lose intensity.'' But we can restore perhaps a few filaments of the mood that possessed him. He would lose, if he remained, the wondrous web of images that shimmered in his mind! He would forget the thoughts that he had laid away, like nuts or winter apples, in the dim chambers of his consciousness! He would sink into a dull conformity with the cautious, conventional, commonplace routine of literary Boston. At fifty, at sixty . . . he could see himself, rather stout, a little shabby, his arm laden with parcels, waiting at the corner of Boylston Street for the Cambridge horse-car, his mind running on a new serial, another ''old New England story'' for the *Atlantic*. . . . Shades of Balzac and the world forgone! The world, alas, the great, the dangerous, the delightful world!

The recurring theme of James's first period as a novelist was to be that ''hatred of tyranny'' of which Mr. Ezra Pound speaks, that defence of ''human liberty, personal liberty, the rights of the individual against all sorts of intangible bondage.'' His novels, Miss Bosanquet observes, are "a sustained and passionate plea for the fullest freedom of the individual development that he saw continually imperilled by barbarian stupidity." Who that recalls *The Bostonians*, that picture of a world which seems to consist of nothing but hands, manipulating, repressing, reproving, pushing, pulling, exploiting hands, can doubt that, in all this, James was inspired by the sacred terror of his own individuality? The characters in his early novels are not as a rule quite sure of what they want in Europe, though they all exist for the sake of getting there. What they are sure of is that they want to escape from America—and they never do quite escape: the "strange inevitable tentacles" that James himself still felt as a man of seventy are always trying to drag them back. Hands reach for them over the sea; their friends pursue them; peremptory letters follow them, imploring them to return. Who can forget Isabel Archer's efforts to shake off those importunate well-wishers, Henrietta Stackpole and Casper Goodwood, who are always reminding her of her "old ideals" and of her proper destiny as a "bright American girl"? Or the letters that follow the young painter Singleton, appealing to him as "son, brother, fellow-citizen"? Or Roderick Hudson's family, watching him from across the ocean, ever ready to intervene if he makes what they consider a false step? Or, to go forward to *The Ambassadors*, Strether's attempt to get Chad back from Paris, and Mrs. Newsome's attempt to get Strether? From the first page of *The Ambassadors* to the last, one seems to feel that ship, waiting, under full steam, in Boston Harbor, to speed away at a moment's notice and fetch Strether home. And what does America signify to these characters? *The destiny of Jim Pocock,* to put it in a phrase, vulgarization, that is to say, brutalization, the eclipse of all their finest possibilities: Strether, we recall, hopes that Jim Pocock will come to Paris—it will so clearly reveal to Chad the sort of life to which they are all trying to induce him to return.

Can one doubt that in these fables James was expressing his own fears? . . . But let me make one further observation. Jim Pocock's face is the same face of horror that Spencer Brydon encountered when the ghost of his American self dropped its hands.

CHAPTER III

"IT'S a wretched business," said Roderick Hudson, "this virtual quarrel of ours with our own country, this everlasting impatience that so many of us feel to get out of it. Can there be no struggle then, and is one's only safety in flight?" This was the great question which, for a dozen years, had filled the horizon of Henry James. Later, in his life of Story, he was to speak of it as an inward drama that has enacted itself in thousands of breasts and thousands of lives. "There is often," he adds, in the same connexion, "a conflict of forces as sharp as any of those in which the muse of history, the muse of poetry, is usually supposed to be interested."

For several years he had been travelling uneasily back and forth between Europe and America. "The great fact for us all there [at home]," he writes in a letter from Florence, in 1874, "is that, relish Europe as we may, we belong much more to that than to this, and stand in a much less factitious and artificial relation to it." Beyond everything else there was one consideration that must have weighed heavily with him: the writers he most admired were saturated with the atmosphere of their own countries. Of Turgenev he ob-

48

serves: "His works savor strongly of his native soil, like those of all great novelists." Like the works of Balzac, for example, the greatest of his masters, like the works of George Eliot and George Sand, like those even of Flaubert, Zola, Daudet, Maupassant, whom he was to meet, with whom he was to talk, and who were to reveal to him so many of the secrets of the craft. Could one advance very far as a novelist without that particular saturation? There was Hawthorne, his own American Hawthorne: what light did Hawthorne throw upon this perplexing question? A light, alas, that was anything but reassuring. Hawthorne, James was obliged to remark, "forfeited a precious advantage in ceasing to tread his native soil. Half the virtue of *The Scarlet Letter* and *The House of the Seven Gables* is in their local quality: they are impregnated with the New England air." One had only to consider *The Marble Faun* beside these works! "He has described the streets and monuments of Rome with a closeness which forms no part of his reference to those of Boston and Salem. But for all this he incurs that penalty of seeming factitious and unauthoritative which is always the result of an artist's attempt to project himself into an atmosphere in which he has not a transmitted and inherited property." Disturbing thoughts for a young novelist at the cross-roads!

Yes; with the examples of all these other novelists in his mind, Henry James was aware that he had much at stake. Not for nothing, in spite of his fears, had he given his own country a "good trial": all the great novelists had had worlds to interpret, it was necessary to have one's world, and had any one ever heard of a novelist—a serious novelist—whose world was not the matrix of his own inherited instincts? Linger as one might in fancy over this or that alien paradise, could one ever be anything else than the child of one's own people, could one truly engraft oneself upon another civilization, engraft oneself so completely as to assimilate it and live it and re-live it and create from it? Possibly; conceivably. Still, how much one would have to risk! At the lowest estimate, one would have as it were to be born again; one would have to undergo a second education; one would have to learn the ropes of life anew; one would have to acquire by study, by concentrated effort, those innumerable elements of the soul of a people which the native absorbs with his mother's milk. Oh, one could make up stories as readily about England or France as about the land of Cockaigne! But to express the genius of the race in the manner of the masters—was *that* compassable? How easily one might succeed only in losing one's own world without gaining any other! How easily one might expend all one's energy in the preliminary effort to grasp one's material! And one would be working quite without precedent, one would be leaping in the dark. . . .

These thoughts, we may be sure, presented themselves in their full force to the mind of Henry James. They must inevitably have arisen out of the situation in which he found himself and of which the two outstanding elements were that he dreamed of being a novelist after the pattern of the greatest and that he stood in the most equivocal of relationships to the society in which he had been born. They pressed upon his troubled consciousness: at least, it is difficult to explain otherwise why, as Mr. Lubbock puts it, "the satisfaction of his wish"—to return to Europe—"was delayed for as long as it was." He had ample means, and "his doubtful health," as Mr. Lubbock says, "can hardly have amounted to a hindrance, and the authority of his parents was far too light and sympathetic to stand in his way." He had seen that he could not so easily relinquish his heritage, that he must make every effort to find himself in relation to the society that had formed his instincts and that stood behind him as an infinite prolongation of his own deepest self, that some profound principle, so to speak, of the novelist's life was involved in his ambiguous position. A principle? Why was it that Dostoevsky had crushed in himself a similar dream of going to live in Europe when he perceived that in Europe he became "less Russian," when he realized that he was "capable of being absorbed by Europe"? And why was it that Turgenev returned to Russia, for a "strengthening bath," every summer, to the end of his life? And what was the significance of Renan's remark that a world lived in Turgenev and spoke through his lips, that generations of ancestors, lost and speechless in the slumber of the ages, found in him life and utterance? "The silent spirit of collective masses," said Renan, in that wonderful valedictory to the body of his Russian friend, "is the source of all great things." The great writer is the voice of his own people: *that* was the principle, the principle of which every European novelist of the first order had been a living illustration, and James had been too intelligent not to perceive it. *Il faut vivre, combattre et finir avec les siens!* And he had lingered, he had waited, he had hesitated . . . and it had been quite useless. A fixed idea had prevented him from throwing himself into the life that he feared, and that life, which he had never challenged, had grown more formidable every day. Was it a choice between losing one's soul and losing one's senses, between surviving as a spiritual cripple and not surviving at all? In any case, principle or no principle, there was only one course open to him: he must escape. And as for principles, had any one ever yet explored all the possibilities of the literary life?

It is improbable that James clearly formulated in his own mind the possible consequences of his action. It is certain, on the other hand, that what he felt, on his return to Europe, was an immense relief, an immense delight. He had crossed the Alps in 1869, and "the wish—the absolute sense of need—to see Italy again" had oppressed him during the following year at home. He had come back, to Rome, to Florence, to Venice, before he had at last settled in Paris; he had come back, and with what sensations! Had he not grasped there, truly grasped, "what might be meant by the life of art"? Those elements of accumulation in the human picture, those infinite superpositions of history, those fragments of the festal past! Those mellowed harmonies of tint and contour, those clustered shadows amid the ruins! And the starlit nights at Florian's, and the rides on the Campagna, and the rambles over the Tuscan

countryside, with a volume of Stendhal in one's pocket!
. . . "I have come on a pilgrimage," says the hero of
one of his early stories. "To understand what I mean,
you must have lived, as I have lived, in a land beyond
the seas, barren of romance and grace. This Italy of
yours, on whose threshold I stand, is the home of history, of beauty, of the arts—of all that makes life
splendid and sweet. . . . Here I sit for the first time in
the enchanted air in which love and faith and art and
knowledge are warranted to become deeper passions
than in my own chilly clime. I begin to behold the
promise of my dreams. . . . The air has a perfume;
everything that enters my soul, at every sense, is a suggestion, a promise, a performance." . . . James's own
salute—was it not?—to the "sublime synthesis" of
Europe.

But Italy had not held him. He had fairly reeled
through the streets of Rome in a fever of enjoyment.
Rome, Florence, Venice: Italy and youth, youth and, if
not love, at least moonlight—he had known them all.
But he had had his wits about him; he had been sys-
tematic in the midst of his ecstasies; he had been alert.
He had written *Roderick Hudson* during those months,
and not for himself had fate and a forewarning conscience predestined such a career as that luckless
artist's! He had known sweet, full, calm hours, hours
in which everything in him had been stilled and absorbed in the steady perception of that wondrous panorama. In those venerable cities how life had revelled
and postured in its strength! How sentiment and passion had blossomed and flowered! What a wealth of

mortality had ripened and decayed! His æsthetic sense had seemed for the first time to live a sturdy creative life of its own. Yet something had always been amiss there; it was, after all, a museum-world—one lingered at one's peril. Had he not found in Rome the relics, the remnants of the ancient American group—"much broken up, or rather broken down"—Story's, even Hawthorne's group, that little circle of easy artistry and sociability which had had its high moments, moments of Mazzini, moments of the Brownings, and had listened so long to the sirens that the slow years had lapped it round and left it there, a shadow, an echo, a dream? That, in the golden air, was the doom of the American artist! And as for "Italian life," how could one ever grasp it? Italy, for an alien, was like some strange, iridescent shell-fish in the hands of a child: the living organism lurked too far within, and the shell was irre-frangible, and the shape and the color were so entrancing that one forgot everything else. Had not Hawthorne, with all his perseverance and all his magic, shown just how helpless, in such conditions, the American novelist was? . . . No, Italy was the casket of gold, but the treasure was not hidden there. He must try the silver casket next, and then the casket of lead.

It was to Paris that James repaired when, at thirty-two, he left America for good, and "it does not seem to have occurred to him at the time," says Mr. Lubbock, "to seek a European home anywhere else." Nevertheless, he remained in Paris scarcely a year: why did he go there, what did he gain from his year's adventure, and why did he leave so soon? Between the lines of his

letters and his essays we seem to discern the story: to
the end of his life James was to look back upon this
year as, in a certain sense, his *annus mirabilis*. For
Paris had indeed been the second, the more essential,
nursery of his intellect: what secrets he had learned
there, secrets of the craft that he was never to forget!
He had always known that art lives upon discussion,
upon experiment, upon curiosity, upon variety of attempt, upon the exchange of views and the comparison
of standpoints; he had always felt that the best things
come, as a general thing, from the talents that are
members of a group. And there in Paris he had been
welcomed by the Olympians themselves—by Flaubert
and Turgenev. Welcomed? Yes. It was true that
they had shown little interest in his own work: they
had found it—had they not?—*proprement écrit,* but
terribly pale. The gentle giant from the steppes had
even suggested that it had on the surface too many
little flowers and knots of ribbon, that it was not quite
meat for men. That was a pity: one liked to be appreciated. Still, he had come to Paris, in all piety, for
quite another purpose; he had come to learn, and what
surprising opportunities he had encountered! Madame
Viardot's Sunday evenings had not been very amusing,
since he had no ear; but he had met Turgenev there,
not *always* on all fours in the act of presenting some
extravagant charade. And he had fairly taken possession of the Théâtre Français: he had had his precious
moments even behind the scenes, behind the veil of the
temple of decorum. And there had been mornings at
Auteuil, in Edmond de Goncourt's study, odorous with

the enchanting smell of old books and thronged with
articles of virtu, redolent of the eighteenth century.
Best of all, there had been Flaubert's Sunday afternoons.   He had heard the old master discourse upon
Hugo and recite, with his beautiful accent, the sonnets
of Gautier; and he had met the disciples there, Goncourt
again, straight and tall, with his pointer-like nose and
his sharp glance, Zola, pale and sombre, and the indefatigable Daudet, and Guy de Maupassant, still *inédit,*
with his fantastic tales, Maupassant the never absent,
the apple of the master's eye.   What conversation!
Could one ever, in the long future, hope to hear its like
again?

Memories indeed, guardian memories, memories to
store away in one's mind, in one's conscience, against
the famine years to come!   Thick-witted England would
never provide such a feast for one's insatiable craftsman's appetite.   These besotted mandarins, with their
truly infernal intelligence of art, form, manner: well,
theirs was the only work that one would ever be able to
respect.   They spoiled one for the English style—save
the mark!—the puffy, stuffy, hasty, padded three-decker,
informe, ingens, which those amiable islanders slapped
together and tossed into the face of the public.   Who
could forget Flaubert's thundering objurgations on that
unendurable English lack of the sense of design?   Design, *plan*—that was the uppermost idea in every mind
at those councils at which one had assisted, silently, in
one's corner—listening, while the Olympians, old and
young, with what passion and what conviction, and how
systematically and articulately, exchanged their **free**

confidences on the work of the day, on the pusillanimity, the superficiality, the vulgarity of those who were *not* Olympians, and on their own schemes and ambitions. Lightness and shapeliness, grace and felicity in style, lucidity, logic, the clear image, the just word, the precise observation: true, these were the arts with which to cultivate one's own garden. Counsels of artistic perfection —he had gathered an inexhaustible store.

Yes, it had been the most wonderful of years. And yet, it was strange, he had come to Paris with the idea perhaps of passing his life there, and within a year he had wearied of it all. He had found himself surfeited with the French mind and its utterance. And why? He had been welcomed by the Olympians, in a sense; but really welcomed? Had there not been abysses of mental reservation on both sides? He had been privileged to listen: that was the truth of the matter. He had had only to put in a rash word to be reminded that his place was below the salt. Even Flaubert, the huge, the diffident, the courteous and accessible Flaubert, had abused him, unmercifully, when he had presumed to make some depreciatory comment on the style of Prosper Mérimée. They were so hostile and exclusive, at bottom, these Olympians; they positively preaccepted such a degree of interest in their own behalf. Even Turgenev, whom they so much admired, had remarked that the French recognized no originality whatever in other peoples, that, apart from their own affairs, they were interested in nothing, they knew nothing. They were the people in the world whom one had to go more of the way to meet than to meet any other, and did they sufficiently requite one's effort? Did their conversation, on such terms, and beyond a certain point, compensate for that ruthless abrogation of one's *amour-propre?* One adored them as craftsmen, but otherwise? They were ignorant and complacent: they would discuss by the hour some trifle of Daudet's while they neither knew nor cared what the great George Eliot was doing across the Channel. Yes, and they were corrupt! Turgenev felt that also; quiet aristocrat that he was, he had been disgusted, again and again, by their cynicism; he had never felt at ease in the atmosphere of the Magny dinners. Flaubert was out of the picture most of the time; he was in Paris only for a few months in the winter; and with the younger men one simply could not become intimate. Was it possible that he had come to Paris too late, that he would have been more at home there in the old romantic days? If he had grown up in France . . . if he had been still in his twenties. . . . It was impossible now; and besides, there was something so harsh and metallic about these naturalists, who dissected the human organism with the obscene cruelty of medical students, to whom nothing, or rather everything, everything but art, was common and unclean, whose talk savored only of the laboratory and the brothel. Ah, one's tender dreams of Europe, the soft illusion, the fond hope—was *this* what lay behind the veil? Perish the profane suggestion!

Such appear to have been James's sensations, face to face with the literary Paris of 1876. He loved it and hated it, he was at once fascinated and shocked by it. He had felt himself for the first time on his mettle; his perception had been excited to the highest pitch. Never was he to forget the "sharp contagion" of that superior air, the mysteries of which he had been a witness. But that was not all: if his artistic sensibilities had been stimulated, his social and moral sensibilities had been outraged, his pride had been wounded, his romantic vision of Europe had suffered a cruel wrong. Such later reminiscences as we find here and there in his *Notes on Novelists,* for example, tell us very little about his real feelings at the time: it is from his writings of the 'seventies, from the general view of life revealed in those writings, and from the scattered reports one has gathered of his private conversation, that his true attitude is to be discerned. Mr. Hueffer, for instance, tells us that he cherished for Flaubert, in reality, a "lasting, deep rancor," that he "hated" him, that he referred again and again to Flaubert as having abused him in the discussion of Mérimée, that he could never forgive the master for having opened his own door in a dressing-gown, and would talk of the other writers he had met "not infrequently in terms of shuddering at their social excesses," that he would relate "unrepeatable stories of the *ménages* of Maupassant." Turn to his own writings of the time, or of the years immediately preceding it. Had he not, in one of his reviews, reproved Swinburne for not striking the moral note or betraying the smallest acquaintance with the conscience? Had he not summed up his admiration for George Eliot by saying that her touchstone was "the word respectable"? In these writings of his own, as in these reports of his conversation, we distinguish at least a few of the "fifty reasons" why, as he wrote to Howells, he could not become intimate with the literary fraternity of Paris or even "like their wares." He had fled from Boston, but he had retained, as we see, the stamp of his own ancestral Puritan world.

No, he had not been able to stomach these ferocious companions, not for long. But how he had acclaimed their ideas, how he had marvelled at their way of doing the very things that he had so seldom been able to like! He who had reproved Swinburne for not striking the moral note had also reproved Browning for his neglect of form; he had remarked, in another review and on the same grounds, that it was "an offence against humanity" to place Dickens among the greatest novelists; and he had been repelled by Rubens because of his wastefulness, his "careless grasp." He had been ready, in short, for this Gallic evangel of design, economy, method, and with what rapture he had embraced it! And there was something else that he owed to these mandarins, something a little painful, but at the same time infinitely exhilarating. Why had he listened to them so silently, so breathlessly? Had he not felt himself at a disadvantage, he who had waited so long in that far-away America, hesitating, irresolute, chafing to be off, he who was no longer a child and who had lost perhaps a little of his original capacity to adapt himself, to respond fully to this eagerly anticipated opportunity? How assured these men seemed, even the youngest of them: it was as if they had been born veterans of the craft. And what pacemakers they were! How disconcerting, and at the same time how enlivening! He had been stirred to a passion of emulation, a "rage of determination," as he was to call it later, "to *do,* and triumph."

Fear—if we must go back to that—fear had given him wings. "There were 'movements' he was too late for," Strether is conceived as thinking in *The Ambassadors;* "weren't they, with the fun of them, already spent? There were sequences he had missed and great gaps in the procession; he might have been watching it all recede in a golden cloud of dust." Strether was middle-aged when at last he found his way to Paris; but had not James himself shared and remembered that sensation of being perhaps too late? Had he not always felt that the great life, the creative life, was a European secret, that it was almost open to question whether an American could be an artist at all? "We are the disinherited of art!" says Theobald in *The Madonna of the Future.* "We are condemned to be superficial. We are excluded from the magic circle. The soil of American perception is a poor little barren, artificial deposit. Yes! we are wedded to imperfection. An American, to excel, has just ten times as much to learn as a European. We lack the deeper sense: we have neither taste, nor tact, nor force. How should we have them? Our crude and garish climate, our silent past, our deafening present, the constant pressure about us of unlovely circumstance, are as void of all that nourishes and prompts and in-spires the artist as my sad heart is void of bitterness in saying so! We poor aspirants must live in perpetual exile." How many times, in hours of doubt, James must have shared these misgivings! One thing is clear: he was convinced that he had a long inheritance to make amends for, that he must win what others had by right of birth. "He could never forget," as Mr. Lubbock says, "that he had somehow to make up to himself for arriving as an alien from a totally different social climate: for his own satisfaction he had to wake and toil while others slept."

The traces of this intense preoccupation are to be found everywhere in his early writings. "I believe in you," says Rowland Mallet to Roderick Hudson, as they set out for Europe, "if you are prepared to work and to wait and to struggle and to exercise a great many virtues." And again: "For heaven's sake, if you have got facility, revere it, respect it, adore it, hoard it— don't speculate on it." But aside from such mere fragments of dialogue as these, how does it happen that so many of James's characters are represented as having on their hands some more or less gifted protégé whose education is their principal object in life? His first novel, *Watch and Ward*, describes the bringing up of Nora, the exotic little Western waif, by her future husband Roger Lawrence. *Roderick Hudson* is largely the story of Rowland's endeavor to keep his extravagant young friend in the strait path of self-development. In *The Tragic Muse*, Sherringham devotes himself to educating Miriam Rooth for the stage, while Gabriel Nash's function in life seems to consist in serving as a sort of conscience for Nick Dormer. And there is *The Bostonians*, the theme of which is the struggle between Ransome and Olive Chancellor for the tutelage of Verena Tarrant. Do we not distinguish, in the continual recurrence of this motif, the vestiges of James's own absorption in the problem of educating himself? These char-

acters are all engaged in remodelling one another, in
preparing one another for a career that involves infinite
difficulties, a career that is beset with dangers; and as
we glance at the *Notes of a Son and Brother,* at the
passage on John La Farge, we seem to discern the
thought that lay at the bottom of James's mind. Many
were the incentives that led to the development of that
steely will of his. There was the pledge that he had
virtually taken to make up in his work for having missed
the war. And how keenly he must have felt the necessity
of justifying his expatriation! We can see in his letters
how conscious he was of the eyes of Cambridge, not to
mention Boston and the "Higginsonian fangs." But
to return to La Farge and those earlier days at Newport:
La Farge was "of the type—the 'European,' " he remarks, "and this gave him an authority for me that it
verily took the length of years to undermine." And
what had been La Farge's counsel to a fellow-American
who had been presumptuous enough also to dream of the
life of art? "The artist's serenity"—so James inter-
preted it—"was an intellectual and spiritual capital
that must never brook defeat—which it so easily might
incur by a single act of abdication." And again:
"There was no safety or, otherwise, no inward serenity
or even outward—though the outward came secondly—
unless there was no deflection." *No deflection!* The
European artist, rejoicing in his strength and his abun-
dant resources, might permit himself an occasional lapse
from the strait and narrow path, the American did so
at his peril: for him a single act of abdication might
signify the end of all things. "It's a complex fate,

being an American," James wrote in a letter of 1872, "and one of the responsibilities it entails is fighting against a superstitious valuation of Europe." That was the great battle of James's life, and who can deny that he lost it? But the extremity of the artist was the opportunity of the craftsman, and we cannot but trace to this humility the dogged perseverance that was to make him one of the great workers of literary history.

Meanwhile, to return to Paris, he had been faced with the problem of discovering a possible terrain. He had tried to take the measure of his difficulties: he had watched himself as Rowland watches Roderick—"as my mother at home watches the tea-kettle she has set to boil." Never had a man more thriftily learned the art of nursing his own talent: he was in danger, had he but known it, of one thing only, the cutting off at their source of the headsprings of experience. But now a great practical problem had risen before him: if he was to abandon America he must have another field, and where was that field to be found? . . . There was, to be sure, the world of his fellow-expatriates, the little world of the "colonies" and the tourists who, like himself, were adrift in Europe. The Henrietta Stackpoles, the Daisy Millers, the Christopher Newmans—how vastly amusing they were! He saw them with the acute receptivity of a fellow-voyager, so to speak, on shipboard: does one ever see people quite so acutely, quite so memorably, as in that relation? And he understood them by the deep law of racial affinity. How startling was the contrast between these innocents abroad and the ornate, the established background against which they moved and shifted! And how well prepared he was to enter into their "predicament," their thoughts and their sensations! But after all he possessed here a very limited domain; he could survey it, he could grasp it in all its aspects, in a few months—and what then? Did not this parasitical world indeed presuppose, as it were, and all but inevitably pass one on to the "host" upon which it lived? It could not serve him for ever as a subject; he must have a more substantial, a more permanent world to represent. And in which direction was he to turn?

He found himself excluded on every side. "I feel for ever how Europe keeps holding one at arm's length," he wrote in one of his letters home, "and condemning one to a meagre scraping of the surface." And again: "What is the meaning of this destiny of desolate exile— this dreary necessity of having month after month to do without our friends for the sake of this arrogant old Europe which so little befriends us?" He had tested Italy, and he had found no one but "washerwomen and waiters," as he remarks, to talk to, waiters and sacristans and language-masters whom he had had to pay for their conversation. Where was the great world upon which his heart was set, or, rather, how was he to penetrate it? "Even a creature addicted as much to sentimentalizing as I am over the whole *mise-en-scène* of Italian life," he observes, "doesn't find an easy initiation into what lies behind it." And what, in sum, had even France yielded him? "A good deal of Boulevard and third-rate Americanism; few retributive relations otherwise." The Continent was closed to him. "I wondered of course who lived in them, and how they lived, and what was society in Altdorf," says the narrator of another of his early stories, referring to the old burgher mansions in a Swiss town through which he is passing; "longing plaintively, in the manner of roaming Americans, for a few stray crumbs from the native social board; with my fancy vainly beating its wings against the great blank wall, behind which, in travel-haunted Europe, all gentle private interests nestle away from intrusion. Here, as elsewhere, I was struck with the mere surface-relation of the Western tourist to the soil he treads. He filters and trickles through the dense social body in every possible direction, and issues forth at last the same virginal water-drop. 'Go your way,' these antique houses seemed to say, from their quiet courts and gardens; 'the road is yours and welcome, but the land is ours. You may pass and stare and wonder, but you may never know us.'" Ah, that arrogant old Europe! Turn where he might, at the native social board there had been no place for James.

"I have done with 'em forever," he wrote to his brother in 1876, "and am turning English all over. I desire only to feed on English life and the contact of English minds—I wish greatly I knew some. Easy and smooth-flowing as life is in Paris, I would throw it over tomorrow for an even very small chance to plant myself for a while in England. If I had but a single good friend in London I would go thither. I have got nothing important out of Paris nor am likely to." But that was an exaggeration. Paris had not given him a field for the exercise of his talent; on the other hand, he had

acquired there a doctrine, a faith, without which he
could hardly have confronted the future at all. He had
grown up artistically under the old dispensation—and
was it false?—in which the novelist was nothing if not
the child of his own people, the voice of his own people.
It was this belief, more than anything else—or so we are
led to assume—that had kept him so long in America;
he had had no warrant to suppose that he could ever
master another world, and his leap to Europe had been
largely a leap in the dark. And here in Paris he had
heard of nothing but "observation": the writer had
ceased to be called a voice, he had become an animated
note-book. Was it not the burden of those conversations
at Flaubert's that one could "get up" any subject, any
field, any world, if one set to work with sufficient system
and lived in one's eyes and one's ears? Had not the
whole Flaubertian brotherhood listened with unqualified
sympathy when Zola set forth the prodigious achieve-
ments of his own sensory organism? . . . To the end
of his life James cherished for Zola a respect that, in
him, we find almost inexplicable save as the result of
some profound impression that he had received in his
youth; and is it not the case indeed that Zola had given
him the cue for which he had been waiting? Was it
true, after all, as Hawthorne had seemed to prove, that
a novelist could not successfully "project himself into
an atmosphere in which he had not a transmitted and
inherited property?" Was it really a fact that one's
"native soil" mattered so very much? Zola denied it—
if not by word, at least by every implication of his doctrine: was he not himself on the very point of "getting

up'' Italy with a Baedeker? . . . To be sure, Zola's
Italy! . . . And it was also true that none of the other
naturalists ventured beyond the limits of France. But
James was not in a position to look too closely into a
faith that seemed to assure his own artistic salvation.
There is a certain truth in Mr. Lubbock's remark that
he went to England ''more by a process of exhaustion
than by deliberate choice'': he could not, he felt, not
yet, turn back to America, and he had found that the
Continent was impracticable. And how his heart leaped
at the thought of England, England on any terms!

CHAPTER IV

THE SIEGE OF LONDON

"IT had rolled over her that what she wanted of Europe was 'people,' so far as they were to be had, and that if her friend really wished to know, the vision of this same equivocal quantity was what had haunted her during their days, in museums and churches, and what was again spoiling for her the pure taste of Scenery. She was all for Scenery, yes; but she wanted it human and personal, and all she could say was that there would be in London—wouldn't there?—more of that kind than anywhere else."

Such were the thoughts of Milly Theale in *The Wings of the Dove,* and Henry James was of the same mind. He wanted "people"—the right people in the right conditions—and where were they to be found save in England? What he, like Milly, had in view was "no thought of society nor of scraping acquaintance"; or rather it was not quite that. "It was the human, the English picture itself—the world imagined always in what one had read and dreamed." Thackeray's world, Trollope's world, the world even of Sir Thomas Lawrence, even of Gainsborough! Where did it begin or end, that "old England that an American loves"—Washington Irving's England, with all that had piled up the soft legend in

the years between? Tone, harmony, order, the stately
offices of life! Tennysonian lawns and elm-scattered
meadows, high-gabled farmhouses and timbered manors!
The adored footpath, the first primroses, the stir and
scent of renascence in the watered sunshine and under
spreading boughs! The names and places and things
which, in the far exile of one's infancy, had become for
one values and secrets and shibboleths! Society? Of
course society was a part of the picture: one had always
conceived of that world as the setting of an incomparable human drama. . . . Yes, the rest, France and
Italy, had been mere scenery: museums and churches.
In England, somehow, one had come back to one's own.

Had he hesitated? Had he felt at times uncertain,
diffident, irresolute, apprehensive? Had he shrunk from
the ordeal that awaited him? It was far from simple.
But how he had longed for this alluring world! Try as
he might he had not been able to escape from its fateful
incantation. Six years before—he was thirty-three now
—he had experienced that first phase of initiation and
wonder in the British paradise: he had had those few
precarious months, months when he had felt as inexor-
able the tug of his American destiny and the whole bliss-
ful scene had given out its message and story as with the
still, collected passion of an only chance. How he had
acclaimed it, feasted upon it, revelled in it! For no
sooner had he entered England than the old spell, the
spell of his childhood, had resumed its sway over him.

Yes, he had recalled to the last intangibility those
miraculous months that had been so painful in their
sweetness. He had told over and over in his mind each

cherished impression: homesickness was a sensation that he had never felt before, but it haunted him now like a passion. He remembered those first hours in Liverpool, at the Adelphi Hotel—how he had observed, absurdly enough, that in England the plate of buttered muffin and its cover were sacredly set upon the slop-bowl after hot water had been ingeniously placed in the latter, and had seen that circumstance in a perfect cloud of accompaniments. And, still at the Adelphi, there had been the incomparable truth to type of the waiter, truth to history, to literature, to poetry, to Dickens, to Thackeray, positively to Smollett and to Hogarth, to every connection that could help one to appropriate him and his setting, an arrangement of things hanging together with a romantic rightness that had the force of a revelation. In short, "recognition" was what had remained, through the adventures of the months that followed, the liveliest principle at work: every face was a documentary scrap, every sound was strong, whether rich and fine or only queer and coarse; everything in this order drew a positive sweetness from never being—whatever else it was— gracelessly flat. And as with objects, faces, voices, so it was with persons: if the commonest London street-vista had been a fairly heart-shaking contributive image, if Craven Street, for example, had positively reeked with associations born of the particular ancient piety embodied in his "private altar" to Dickens, what was to be said of the eminent gentlemen, the accomplished ladies who had received the pilgrim, or whom he had casually met in their drawing-rooms, or against whom he had merely brushed as it were in the vestibule of the temple?

There was George Eliot who had been so kind to a young
spirit almost abjectly grateful, or at any rate all devoutly prepared.   And Charles Darwin, beautifully
benignant, sublimely simple.   And Lady Waterford,
illustrational, historically, precisely so.   And Frederic
Harrison who, young as he was, had yet been referred to
in one of Matthew Arnold's essays: the beauty was thus
at such a rate that people *had* references, and that a
reference was, to *his* mind, whether in a person or an
object, the most glittering, the most becoming ornament
possible.   And finally there was Swinburne whose star
had risen over Boston like a new Lucifer of evil omen:
he had thrilled with the prodigy of the circumstance—
he had been walking through the National Gallery—
that he should have been admiring Titian in the same
breath with Mr. Swinburne—that is, in the same breath
in which Mr. Swinburne had admired Titian and he
had also admired Mr. Swinburne!   It was not merely
that he had caught everywhere the exciting note of a
social order in which everyone wasn't hurled straight,
with the momentum of rising, upon an office or a store:
he had caught that note on the Continent, in France, in
Italy.   Nor was it simply that he had fairly basked in
the light of distinction.   He had felt—there was the
point—that he belonged to this English world, that it
was his by every right of possession.   Had he not lived
in it really, lived, in a sense, from the day when his consciousness had first awakened?   It was his own thought
that James placed in the mouth of his Passionate Pilgrim.   "I had the love of old forms and pleasant rites,"
says Searle, as he sits in Hampton Court, "and I found

them nowhere—found a world all hard lines and harsh lights, without composition, as they say of pictures, without the lovely mystery of color. . . . Sitting here in this old park, in this old country, I feel that I hover on the misty verge of what might have been! I should have been born here, not there! . . . This is a world I could have got on with beautifully." And James, like the disinherited Searle, had come to regain his birthright.

He had come, he had seen, he had been greeted with every cordiality. What souvenirs he was to cherish in after years, souvenirs of this hour when the gates of the paradise of the first larger initiations had opened before him! He could remember—ah, who had remembered such things as these! He had known Lord Houghton, and whom had Lord Houghton not known? He had "breakfasted out" in a day and under circumstances that signified association at a jump with the ghosts of Byron and Sheridan and Scott and Moore and Lockhart and Rogers and *tutti quanti.* He had gossiped with Mrs. Procter, Barry Cornwall's widow, that immemorial, indefatigable, ever-delightful survivor for whom Byron and Sheridan and Rogers and *tutti quanti* had never been ghosts at all. He had heard Mrs. Procter say—for all the world as if the lady in question lived next door— that one "hadn't received" Mrs. Shelley. How illustrational *that* was! What a reference! And he had ridden to Mrs. Procter's funeral, in the same coach with Browning and Kinglake. Browning had read to him, Gladstone had talked to him, Mrs. Kemble had welcomed him; and there had been Ruskin and Huxley and Herbert Spencer —not that he had wished to fill his bucket at *those* wells!

Yes, he had seen Shelley plain, all the Shelleys, for Shelleys they all were: celebrated, gifted, remote, and at once great themselves and friends of the great. How much he had owed to Lowell and the endlessly ministering Charles Norton—Norton, with his genius for friendship, Norton, the confidant of so many of the deities, Norton and especially Lowell, the supereminent ambassador, with whom, in whatever company, he had been able to repose in a golden confidence! He had come just in time to see the old order stretching back—he had seen faces, faces of Lawrence, faces of Romney, faces, positively—why beat about the bush?—of Raphael. Oh, the charm of talk with those really distinguished women of the past! Nor was it only the old order that he had seen: he had had his lucky share, from the very first, of the freedom and ease of the new. Many had been the lurking springs at light pressure of which particular vistas had begun to recede for him, great luminous, furnished, peopled galleries, sending forth gusts of agreeable sound.

Thus Henry James was to retrace these earlier English hours, hours that invested themselves in his recollection with a light as of setting suns. How he had rejoiced in his doom of inordinate exposure to appearances, aspects, images! He had fairly staggered, in his bedazzled state, under the load of his impressions.

Meanwhile, to project our small glass backward, what figure does he present to us as he moves—sedately, watchfully, with an air of reserve and deprecation and a manner, as Mr. Gosse recalls it, a little formal and frightened, in and out of those drawing-rooms, innumer-

able as the chambers of the Vatican, in which for so
many years so much of his life is to be passed? What
are his meditations? He is convinced that, so far as
experience goes, any penetration of the London scene
will *be* experience, after a fashion that no exercise of
one's mere intellectual curiosity wherever else could
begin to represent. Out of doors in foreign lands—Miss
Henrietta Stackpole had not been the first to remark it
—one seemed to see the right side of the tapestry; out
of doors in England one seemed to see the wrong side,
which gave one no notion of the pattern. But indoors,
or even within the gates—for at those wonderful old
country-houses indoors really began at the gates—what
an enchanting drama enacted itself from one year's end
to another! Had he not felt from the first that the
country-house was the clew to almost everything that
was distinctively British? There were aspects, there
were appanages that at times seemed even more
"the thing" than the thing itself. Dower-houses, for
instance . . . *Plash* . . . their very names were quaint
and old. The conditions nowhere so asserted their difference from the conditions of Boston as they appeared
to assert it in these retreats which, few and comparatively simple, scant and even humble as their appoint-
ments occasionally were, implied so many other things
of the sort he had had to tackle. How intensely and
immutably "property" they seemed! And as for the
iniquity—for one couldn't approve of the custom of the
expropriation of the widow in the evening of her days—
well, one's condemnation of this wrong forgot itself
when so many of the consequences looked right, barring

a little dampness: which was the fate sooner or later of most of one's unfavorable judgments of English institutions. Iniquities in such a country somehow always made pictures, and they had not as a general thing prevented the occupation of these delectable sanctuaries by old ladies with unimaginable reminiscences and rare voices, whose reverses had not deprived them of a great deal of becoming hereditary lace. But if the dower-houses were the thing, the country-houses were the *real* thing . . . Summersoft, ah, Summersoft and Matcham, and the pageant there! One had perhaps a tendency to figure these people as larger than life, but, frankly, weren't they? One didn't need—nor did they —to do anything: it was enough for them to exist and for oneself to be there. One had only to watch them to receive an impression or an accession, to feel a relation or a vibration. Had happy time in its rounds ever paused amid comelier scenes?

Henry James looked again, lost himself in his favorite diversion of watching face after face. This amusement gave him the keenest pleasure he knew. Everything was great, of course, in great pictures, and it was doubtless precisely a part of the brilliant life—since the brilliant life, as he had faintly pictured it, clearly *was* humanly led—that all impressions within its area partook of its brilliancy. At dinner, perhaps, above all: the smallest things, the faces, the hands, the jewels of the women, the sound of words, especially of names, across the table, the shape of the forks, the arrangement of the flowers, the attitude of the servants, the walls of the room, were all touches in a picture and denotements

in a play. All these people seemed so completely made
up, so unconscious of effort, so surrounded with things
to rest upon; the men with their clean complexions, their
well-hung chins, their cold, pleasant eyes, their shoulders
set back, their absence of gesture, the women, half
strangled in strings of pearls, with smooth plain tresses,
apparently looking at nothing in particular, supporting
silence as if it were as becoming as candle-light, yet
talking a little sometimes in fresh, rich voices. It was
true that the imagination, in these halls of art and fortune, was almost inevitably accounted a poor matter; the
whole scene and its participants—it was the same wherever he went—abounded so in pleasantness and picture,
in all the felicities, for every sense, taken for granted
there by the very basis of life, that even the sense most
finely poetic, aspiring to extract the moral, could scarce
have helped feeling itself treated to something of the
snub that affects, when it does affect, the uninvited reporter in whose face a door is closed. These English had
such a mortal mistrust of anything like criticism or keen
analysis, appearing as they did to regard it as a kind of
maudlin foreign flummery! But what of it? Had he
not *come* for an England that would turn its back
directly, and without fear of doing it too much, on
examples and ideas not strictly homebred? There was
enough left, in all conscience, enough at Matcham,
enough at Summersoft, not to mention Newmarch and
Ricks and Covering End—and the universe of London!
Every voice in the great bright circle was a call to the
ingenuities and immunities of pleasure; every echo was
a defiance of difficulty, doubt, or danger; every aspect

of the picture a glowing plea for the immediate. Riddles and charms, marvels and mysteries! Young men with a way that was wonderful of entering a box at ten o'clock in the evening. Door-bells as little electric as possible. Ambiguous military persons in mufti who were unmistakably gentlemen in spite of their seedy coats and trousers. Enchanting ladies whom one heard addressed as "Countess" and "Ma toute-belle." It was their all so domestically knowing one another that mainly struck him—they were as if wrapped in a community of ideas, of traditions. As for London, "my earliest apprehension," says Henry James, "piled up the monster to such a height that I could somehow only fear him as much as I admired and that his proportions in fact reached away quite beyond my expectation. He was always the great figure . . . and I was for no small time, as the years followed, to be kept at my awestruck distance for taking him on that sort of trust."

Such was the nature of our author's approach to the world he had come to conquer. We find in love, as Joubert said, whatever we bring to it; and is there a passion that is not ennobled by admiration and faith? But what was it that James admired, what was it he believed in? England as the English knew it, a world of mere men and women? It was a fairer world than ours, a fairer world than England's, a fairer world than ever existed outside the pages of romance. A worldly world it was indeed—a world of manners; but these manners were heroic, of a noble congruity of which our rude earth has never afforded a counterpart. It was a distillation, that world, of countless novels of which the

last intention of the authors had been to see any object
as in itself it really was and which had formed the
shimmering universe of the little boy in Fourteenth
Street. That was the world he had dreamed of entering, that was the world he had set out to find, that was
the world in which he had hoped to "come into his own"
—as he had "liked betimes to put it for a romantic
analogy with the state of dispossessed princes and wan-
dering heirs." It was not England, England as it was
or had been, though it seemed to be and James believed
that it was. It was an idea, a veritable Platonic idea, an
idea of which the world of reality could never afford
anything but an imperfect copy.

Mysteries of the romantic mind! To the end of his
life, as we know, and in spite of all his disillusionments,
Henry James cherished his original idea of England.
One remembers how in *The Outcry*, that novel of his old
age, the young prince goes to see the contested picture in
the National Gallery and decides that it is a "Monte-
vano pure and simple." Henry James had never convinced himself that a prince of the house of Windsor could
ever be anything but an *arbiter elegantiarum*. Many
were the rumors in this connection to which he must
have been obliged to lend an ear, rumors about Queen
Victoria's "favorite novelist," rumors about the
famous "pleasures" of the Prince of Wales. His intelligence undoubtedly took them in, but something deeper
than his intelligence refused to believe them: queens and
princes were simply not that sort of people, they only
appeared to be so, and if one watched them closely and
waited patiently they would in the end appear to be

what they really were. And was not the same thing true of England? The reality of England was what the novelists had pictured; and if it was always slipping away from itself, misrepresenting itself, becoming something it shouldn't be, something it essentially *wasn't*—well, one could only bide one's time. There came a day, to be sure, when James perceived that England was not this "reality"; in a sense he perceived it from the first, perceived it with all the acumen of his conscious mind. Nevertheless, his desire overrode his intellect; the images that had fixed themselves in the fancy of his childhood prevailed over the actualities that met his eyes; he could not quite believe in the reality of the real. The consequences of this double vision were to manifest themselves in the works of his later life. What concerns us now is the fact of the illusion. James had no sooner crossed the threshold of England than he had passed in his own mind into that sphere of "English society" of which the old romancers had left such alluring representations and from which the dross of human existence, its dust and filth, everything that might have qualified its charm, had been as it were hygienically removed. "One placed young gods and goddesses only when one placed them on Olympus," the novelist John Berridge is conceived as thinking in *The Velvet Glove*, "and it met the case, always, that they were of Olympian race, and that they glimmered for one, at the best, through their silver cloud, like the visiting apparitions in an epic." That had been from the first James's instinctive feeling about the society in which he was thrown. It was clothed in a kind of glory that had its source in his own soul.

We have only to note, as illustrating this, the simple
piety with which so many of the characters in his earlier
English stories turn to the fortunate ones of the earth,
turn, so to put it, as sunflowers turn to the sun. Waterville, in *The Siege of London*, devotes "a good deal of
speculation to the baronial class"; Miss Pynsent is "immensely preoccupied" in the same way; Hyacinth
Robinson is always "letting his imagination wander
among the haunts of the aristocracy." Hyacinth, in
particular—but glance at Hyacinth's aspirations, glance
at them in the light of James's comments on them.
"There was a moment," our author says in the preface
to *The Princess Casamassima*, "when [the London
streets] offered me no image more vivid than that of
some individual sensitive nature or fine mind, some small
obscure intelligent creature whose education should have
been almost wholly derived from them, capable of profit-
ing by all the civilization, all the accumulations to which
they testify, yet condemned to see these things only from
outside—in mere quickened consideration, mere wistful-
ness and envy and despair. It seemed to me I had only
to imagine such a spirit intent enough and troubled
enough, and to place it in presence of the comings and
goings, the great gregarious company, of the more fortunate than himself—all on the scale on which London
could show them—to get possession of an interesting
theme. I arrived so at the history of little Hyacinth
Robinson—he sprang up for me out of the London pave-
ment. To find his possible adventure interesting I had
only to conceive his watching the same public show, the
same innumerable appearances I had watched myself,

and of his watching very much as I had watched." And how had Hyacinth watched—with what sensations? Turn to the novel itself. "He wanted to drive in every carriage, to mount on every horse, to feel on his arm the hand of every pretty woman in the place. . . . These familiar phenomena became symbolic, insolent, defiant, took upon themselves to make him smart with the sense that *he* was out of it. . . . His sense was vivid that he belonged to the class whom the upper ten thousand, as they passed, didn't so much as rest their eyes upon for a quarter of a second. . . . They only reminded him of the high human walls, the deep gulf of tradition, the steep embankments of privilege and dense layers of stupidity which fenced him off from social recognition. And this was not the fruit of a morbid vanity on his part, or of a jealousy that could not be intelligent; his personal discomfort was the result of an exquisite admiration for what he had missed. There were individuals whom he followed with his eyes, with his thoughts, sometimes even with his steps; they seemed to tell him what it was to be the flower of a high civilization." To James's sense these "unanswered questions and baffled passions" are a sign of Hyacinth's "noble blood": deep calls to deep, and this "unfortunate but remarkably organized youth," this illegitimate son of a lord, is conscious of nothing but the paradise of which he has been dispossessed. In real life the last thing that would have occurred to a young man in Hyacinth's position would have been to "roam and wander and yearn" about the gates of that lost paradise: he would have gone to Australia, or vanished into the slums, or con-

tinued with the utmost indifference at his trade of bind-
ing books. But this attitude represents the feeling
of Hyacinth's creator; and it is the expression, as I say,
of a simple piety, of a conception of the great world that
could only exist in a confiding soul, of that "extraordinary American good faith"—shall we call it?—at which
James himself so constantly marvels in his own characters. "No Englishman could have written this," said
Blackwood's reviewer of *The Princess Casamassima.*
"Mr. James knows English society too well to be still
overawed in his own person by the divinity that doth
hedge a 'nobleman.' But he is penetrated by the reality
of the difference—the something sacred, after all, which
lies in the fact of noble blood. We are not always thinking of this difference in the old aristocratic countries;
but Mr. James cannot get it out of his mind." Ah, those
reveries of childhood! Henry James had travelled over
land and sea, known men and cities, watched and
labored, he had become withal the most formidable of
artists; and still the dreams of his prime lurked at the
bottom of his heart. The great world had remained for
him what the world of fairies is for other souls: it was
the unquestionable, the sublime, the world beyond good
and evil. To enter it was to cross the threshold of
Utopia.

One easily understands now that "siege of London"
to which James was to devote so much of the energy of
his middle years—understand it, I mean, as something
more than the mere quest for literary material, as something different from the mere pursuit of social success.
One easily understands, for example, those recollections

of Mr. E. S. Nadal, who was one of Lowell's secretaries at the London Embassy in the 'seventies. "He would tell me," says Mr. Nadal, "that he wanted 'to be taken seriously' by the English; that was a phrase he often made use of. . . . When I happened to speak with some disapprobation of the pursuit by Americans of social success in London in spite of the rudeness encountered from some of the London social leaders, he said, 'I don't agree with you. I think a position in society is a legitimate objection of ambition.' . . . He told me once that he particularly detested 'that excluded feeling.' In the things he wrote about that time," Mr. Nadal continues, "I could see indications that his personal relations with English society were very much in his mind. In *An International Episode* an American woman says that an English woman had said to her, 'In one's own class,' meaning the middle class and meaning also that the American woman belonged to that class. The American woman says that she didn't see what right the English woman had to talk to her in that manner. This was a transcript of an incident he related to me one night when we were walking about the London streets. Some lady of the English middle class, whom he had lately visited in the country, had said to him, 'That is true of the aristocracy, but in one's own class it is different,' meaning, said James, 'her class and mine.' Rather than this, he said he preferred to be regarded as a foreigner."

Ah, those Olympians and their "form," that form which appealed to the finest fibres of appreciation! Their right figure was that of life in irreflective joy and at the highest thinkable level of prepared security and

unconscious insolence. They were unconventional indeed—that was a part of their high bravery and privilege; and would not James, like his own John Berridge,
have given six months' royalties for even an hour of
their looser dormant consciousness? Well, he had come
to England to study these people—as one of them; for if
he *wasn't* an Olympian, couldn't he at least become one?
The "manners of 'Europe' "—that was their code; and
when had he failed to invoke it? He had been scarcely
eleven when his school-friend Louis de Coppet in New
York had given him his first pointed prefigurement of
that ideal. Then there had been his cousin Robert
Temple who had come home to bewilder him at Cambridge, home from unheard-of schools in Scotland and
Switzerland, charged with prodigious "English" impressions and awarenesses, a figure of an oddly civilized
perversity. Had he ever forgotten that apparition, that
surprising witness to the effect of Europe? Had he ever
forgotten, for that matter—he had been nine at the time:
the great Thackeray had called upon his father and
mother, had descended upon the family in Fourteenth
Street, had remarked that he, the little boy in his sheath-
like jacket, would have been addressed in England as
"Buttons"—had he ever forgotten how "queer" he had
suddenly realized they all were? From his earliest conscious hour he had abhorred the thinness, the paleness,
the sharpness, the meagreness, as it seemed to him, of
the American temperament. To be somehow "round"
in one's personal line, to be somehow "rich" in one's
personal composition! He had pursued his standard,
his standard of wit, of grace, of good manners, of

vivacity, of urbanity as devoutly as he had pursued the ideal of art; and now he had the gods themselves to contend with. To disconnect himself from his inheritance, to remodel his personality, to build a more stately mansion for his soul—this had become at last a veritable passion.

Some years later William James wrote to his wife from England: "Harry has covered himself, like some marine crustacean, with all sorts of material growths, rich sea-weeds and rigid barnacles and things, and lives hidden in the midst of his strange heavy alien manners and customs; but these are all but 'protective resemblances,' under which the same dear, old, good, innocent and at bottom very powerless-feeling Harry remains, caring for little but his writing, and full of dutifulness and affection for all gentle things." How well his brother understood the singular portent the world was to know as the later Henry James! Others were to be mystified, as time went on, by those strange heavy alien manners and customs, those rich sea-weeds and rigid barnacles, those material growths with which the simple author of *Daisy Miller* was to cover himself and which were to form gradually the astonishing integument of the "later manner." They were, in fact, at least in their incipiency, as William James perceived in 1889, "protective resemblances"—willed and desired, but protective none the less. The "manner" was to develop as one of those compensatory devices in which the human organism is so fertile; it was to develop according to the law by which birds change their plumage and beasts the color of their skins, by which the snow-bird adapts itself to the altering season and the ermine and the Arctic hare assume the robe of winter. What was it but the witness, on James's part, of a certain "felt inequality of condition" between himself and the idealized earthlings among whom he lived?

Ah, to be transformed into what one loves—to possess it, to become it! . . .

CHAPTER V

IN the story called *The Private Life* the author Clarence Vawdrey is represented as carrying on a double existence. He has indeed, like Dr. Jekyll, two characters, the character that writes and the character that appears in society. "One goes out," says the narrator of the story, "the other stays at home. One is the genius, the other's the bourgeois, and it's only the bourgeois whom we personally know." Here again James describes himself. "Much as he always delighted in sociable communion," says Mr. Lubbock, "all his friends must have felt that at heart he lived in solitude and that few were ever admitted into the inner shrine of his labor."

"There it was nevertheless," Mr. Lubbock continues, "that he lived most intensely and most serenely." And there we must observe him now. He had published in 1875 *A Passionate Pilgrim and Other Tales;* he had written *Watch and Ward* and *Roderick Hudson* in Italy and Cambridge; *The American* had been a fruit of his year in Paris. At the moment of his arrival in England (1876) he had scarcely begun to gather in the harvest of the experience of his childhood and youth. That was to be his task for a decade to come: he was to produce

88

in London chiefly the long series of his American and
international novels and tales, *The Europeans, Daisy
Miller, An International Episode, Washington Square,
The Portrait of a Lady, The Siege of London, Four
Meetings, The Bostonians, The Aspern Papers,* and it
was not till 1890, with the publication of *The Tragic
Muse,* in which for the first time, as he says, he attacked
"a purely English subject on a large scale," that his
first phase was to reach a definite climax. We cannot
hope to characterize all these works. We cannot attempt
to trace the astonishing development of a creative
faculty which, in the course of a dozen years, tran-
scended the simple plot-maker's art of *The American,*
the factitious local-colorism of *Roderick Hudson,* and
rendered itself capable of the serene beauty of *The Portrait of a Lady,* the masterly assurance of *The Bostonians,* the mature perfection of *Washington Square.*
Least of all can we penetrate to the heart of this genius,
account for it, apprehend its secret. The most we can
do is to endeavor to describe certain of its qualities, to
grasp a few of its aspects, to perceive it as it were in
operation. For the rest, can we draw out Leviathan with
a hook, or his tongue with a cord which we let down?
I will not conceal his parts, said the Lord to Job, nor
his power, nor his comely proportion. But who can
open the doors of his face? His scales are his pride, shut
up together as with a close seal.

As the Lord abashed Job, so genius abashes the critic.
Who can enter into the springs of the sea of personality?
Let us seek merely to observe our author at his writing-
table, to experience a few of the sensations that animate

him, to share some of the thoughts that ascend from the obscure regions of his inner being. What images, what central vision do we perceive coursing through his brain as he sits, a "bearded Buddha," pen in hand, amid the flooding daylight of his Kensington flat, as he walks, the stockiest of apparitions, but with something vague in the bushiness of his head—an apparition indeed!—as he saunters, with his devouring eye, through the darkening streets? A world has come to birth in his soul, a world no other mind has contemplated. Who are these people that rise before him in a blazing actuality, rise like flowers, like bitter herbs, in the fat soil of a well-nurtured garden? They are the citizens of a domain of which he is the Prospero. Christopher Newman, Daisy Miller, Isabel Archer, Olive Chancellor, Ralph Touchett, Catherine Sloper, Gilbert Osmond, Verena Tarrant: are they parts of himself, these marvellous creatures? Are they selves that he has dreamed of being, longed to be or feared to be, selves to which he is on the point of giving the *coup de grâce* by endowing them with an external existence? They are his, at least, his in their individuality, his in their community, for innumerable ties unite them. He is their master, their principle of life, the force that moves them all.

"Who is Madame Bovary?" said Flaubert. "She is myself." Shall we insist that all the vital characters in the world of fiction are projections of the "selves" of their authors, of aspects of that Protean creature which every creative personality is? How can we know this? How can we say it? But we are justified perhaps in asserting with Maupassant that a writer cannot explain the springs of action of anyone who is remote in character from himself, in believing with Vernon Lee that the most convincing figures in fiction are those which "to all appearance have never been previously analyzed or rationally understood by the author" but rather, "connected always by a similar emotional atmosphere, have come to him as realities, realities emotionally borne in upon his innermost sense." To this is due that intimacy of presentation, that freedom and spontaneity, that zest in treatment which are characteristic of all the master novelists and appear so markedly in this early world of James. He has inherited Washington Square, he has grown up with the Bostonians, he has shared from his infancy the dreams of the "European" American! Catherine Sloper is the cousin of his own cousins, if not by blood at least by the associations of the little circle of his childhood. But glance at these other characters: are they not all related to him in a similar fashion—as facets, so to speak, of his own multiple psyche, the psyche that has been formed by his heredity, by his environment, by his desires, his fears, his sympathies, his antipathies, by everything which, whatever its source, has lodged in the secret places of his being? Olive Chancellor is the quintessence of the dry, predacious Boston that he has watched with the horrified fascination of a young man who feels that his right to live his own life has been menaced—the Boston that insists upon subjecting the impulses of the free individual to the reign of its own provincial law. And how many of his "selves" have escaped to Europe! Roderick Hudson is the artist who has come to fill his pitcher at the fountain.

Christopher Newman is the man who has dreamed of entering the great world and who has been somehow rebuffed. Gilbert Osmond is the "sterile dilettante" from whom James has taken warning, the dilettante of whom he has felt the germs in his own being. Who that has crossed the threshold of this world and stood in the presence of its inhabitants would ever ask for the credentials of its creator or question the degree of his saturation? It is his by a sort of divine right, by the right of instinctive perception, personal experience, absolute knowledge. He has taken notes indefatigably, but these notes have served merely to establish in his consciousness facts that have already existed as it were in the depths of himself. People, his own people—they crowd, they jostle one another in his imagination. Each person has a story, but the story comes to him as a consequence of the qualities of the person: he has no interest in preconceived situations. To give, as Turgenev gave it, the impression of life itself, and not of an arrangement, a *réchauffé* of life: that is his desire. And "the form," he feels, "is to be appreciated after the fact."

The fact. He is a historian, a historian of manners. He is never to relinquish this rôle which is that of all the novelists he admires; he is never to relinquish his belief that "the novel is history" and that "the air of reality (solidity of specification) is the merit on which all its other merits helplessly and submissively depend." The fact obsesses him: it has called into play all his knowledge of form. With what grace, what lightness and purity he has learned to transmit his impressions!

Turgenev has shown him how to deal with small groups of characters, isolated and analyzed; Flaubert has taught him the art of achieving a certain unity of tone; Daudet has helped him to render the most delicate shades of the actual. But behind these secrets of the trade there is always life; and he regards it as the task of the novelist to find out, to know, to see. He has himself found out, he has known, he has seen: but what does he know? He knows as no one else has known it one of the two or three capital phases of the civilization of his country. Do not ask him if he knows the America that is rooted in the soil, the sober, laborious America of the pioneers, the dim, unconscious, Titanic America that is taking shape in the darkness of the hinterland. His America, no less real, is that of the great towns of the Atlantic seaboard; it is, in particular, the America that lives in the thought, the memory, the expectation of the European world from which it has sprung. The nostalgia for the home of his ancestors of the American who has been liberated from the bondage of necessity, the romantic vision of the Old World that exists in the American heart, the drama of the *émigré* in search of the arts of life—this is his natural domain. He possesses it as truly as Balzac possessed the Paris of the Restoration.

He invented it—he discovered it, that is, for literature. He was the first to become conscious of an actual historic drama that has played its part in countless lives on the stage of two continents. He seized upon this drama, traversed and penetrated it in all its aspects; he distinguished the principal types that were involved in it;

he found in it themes for tragedy, comedy, satire. The American business man who, having made his fortune, sets out in quest of the fortune he has missed; the village artist for whom his own country is too immature to provide a school; the ambitious wife of the captain of industry who is so anxious to discover "the best"; the schoolmistress whose parched imagination has been nourished on photographs of castles and cathedrals; the young girl for whom the idea of Europe is interchangeable with the idea of culture; the colonists, the wanderers, the dilettanti, the lovers of the past—such are these beguiled, unsatisfied, imaginative, aspiring, or merely avid souls whose individual development has outshot in some fashion or other the general development of the civilization to which they belong. "Our people," said Emerson, "have their intellectual culture from one country and their duties from another." This defines the phase of American life of which James is the historian and the poet. An America that is actually simple and primitive is inhabited by Americans who inherit the desires, the social and spiritual needs of a civilization that is complex and mature. Release these people from the compulsions of poverty and custom: they read, they dream, they become aware of a thousand requirements for which the world about them affords no scope. There is little in the past of their own country to give shape to these errant fancies that emerge in their minds already clothed as it were in European forms. And accordingly they set forth, as pilgrims to Zion, seekers of the shrine of culture.

Tragedy, satire, comedy are inherent in the situation.

Tragedy. The crusade is a children's crusade. These crusaders are, in our author's phrase, "almost incredibly unaware of life, as the European order expresses life." They are themselves the creatures of another order; they know nothing of the traditions of the Old World, they are unconscious of the fund of evil that runs in the blood of ancient societies, and they take it for granted that the Europeans among whom they are thrown are as ingenuous as themselves. Thus they expose themselves to the direst misunderstandings or they fall into traps and are victimized. To the end of his life, in various forms, James is to repeat this story: for Isabel Archer is only a lovelier Daisy Miller, and Milly Theale is the shadow of Isabel Archer. But comedy and satire spring from these roots as well. The lady correspondent who is so anxious to rifle the secrets of the aristocracy, the American colonists in Paris who are so certain that the French people should be "kept down," Mrs. Touchett, with her "investments," who has lived abroad so long that she has lost her native tact in matters of etiquette, Mr. Flack, the society reporter—they have only to cross the stage to leave in our minds ineffaceable images. They people the Continent with their wit, their vivacity, their absurdity, their vulgarity, their beauty, their avidity.

We are at Geneva, in the 'seventies, in the days of Baron Tauchnitz, on the terrace of the hotel overlooking the lake. There is a flitting hither and thither of stylish young ladies, a rustling of muslin flounces, a rattle of dance-music, a sound of high-pitched voices. Daisy Miller emerges from the open French window, but the youthful Randolph has preceded her. He has just asked

Winterbourne if they have candy in Italy. Rome. The sky is a blaze of blue and the fountains are plashing in their mossy niches. Roderick Hudson has just arrived: he saunters forth into the streets, his brain the theatre of all the emotions of the young artist who has entered Italy for the first time. Venice, and Miss Bordereau hiding away in the depths of her chamber in the old palazzo the letters of the great poet who was her lover in the dim past. Venice, and little Morgan Moreen, the "pupil," dragged about from city to city by his blowsy and sinister family. The café at Havre, and the little schoolmistress of *Four Meetings,* tricked out of her hard-earned savings at the very gate of this dear old Europe. Florence, and Gilbert Osmond and Pansy, "the ideal *jeune fille* of foreign fiction," an edifying blank, and the Countess Gemini who has been written over in a variety of hands. Paris, and the C. P. Hatches and Mrs. Tristram, and Christopher Newman looking up at the towering wall of the Carmelite convent and deciding that revenge is "really not his game." But what eye can embrace at a glance this incomparable community, more real and coherent than any that exists in the world? It lives and moves and breathes in all its members, lives and moves with the poignancy of actual life.

It has been observed from above, as Lilliput is observed by Gulliver. This mind sees everything as in itself it really is; nothing escapes it, nothing deludes it.

Mrs. Luce had been living in Paris since the days of Louis-Philippe; she used to say jocosely that she was one of the generation of 1830—a joke of which the point was not always taken. When it failed Mrs. Luce used always to explain—"Oh, yes, I am one of the romantics"; her French had never become very perfect.

In two sentences we have the germ of a character-study in full length; we know Mrs. Luce as well as if we had been for years one of her visitors on Sunday afternoons.

The train presently arrived, and Miss Stackpole, promptly descending, proved to be, as Isabel had said, decidedly pretty. She was a fair, plump person, of medium stature, with a round face, a small mouth, a delicate complexion, a bunch of light brown ringlets at the back of her head, and a peculiarly open, surprised-looking eye. The most striking point in her appearance was the remarkable fixedness of this organ, which rested without impudence or defiance, but as if in conscientious exercise of a natural right, upon any object it happened to encounter. It rested in this manner upon Ralph himself, who was somewhat disconcerted by Miss Stackpole's gracious and comfortable aspect, which seemed to indicate that it would not be so easy as he had assumed to disapprove of her. . . . "I don't suppose that you are going to undertake to persuade me that *you* are an American," she said.

Do we need to be told that Miss Stackpole is a militant patriot, a resolute woman of action, a resourceful journalist whom nothing daunts, upon whom nothing is lost, and that in spite of her disregard of certain fine shades we are going to like her?

[Mrs. Farrinder] was a copious, handsome woman, in whom angularity had been corrected by the air of success. . . . You . . . had to feel that Mrs. Farrinder imposed herself. There was a lithographic smoothness about her, and a mixture of the

American matron and the public character. There was something public in her eye, which was large, cold, and quiet; it had acquired a sort of exposed reticence from the habit of looking down from a lecture-desk, over a sea of heads, while its distinguished owner was eulogized by a leading citizen. Mrs. Farrinder, at almost any time, had the air of being introduced by a few remarks. She talked with great slowness and distinctness, and evidently a high sense of responsibility; she pronounced every syllable of every word and insisted on being explicit. If, in conversation with her, you attempted to take anything for granted, or to jump two or three steps at a time, she paused, looking at you with a cold patience, as if she knew that trick, and then went on at her own measured pace. She lectured on temperance and the rights of women; the ends she labored for were to give the ballot to every woman in the country and to take the flowing bowl from every man.

[Selah Tarrant] looked like the priest of a religion that was passing through the stage of miracles; he carried his responsibility in the general elongation of his person, of his gestures (his hands were now always in the air, as if he were being photographed in postures), of his words and sentences, as well as in his smile, as noiseless as a patent hinge, and in the folds of his eternal waterproof. . . . [He] and his companion had strange adventures; she found herself completely enrolled in the great irregular army of nostrum-mongers, domiciled in humanitary Bohemia. It absorbed her like a social swamp; she sank into it a little more every day, without measuring the inches of her descent. . . . She had lived with long-haired men and short-haired women, she had contributed a flexible faith and an irremediable want of funds to a dozen social experiments, she had partaken of the comfort of a hundred religions, had followed innumerable dietary reforms, chiefly of the negative order, and had gone of an evening to a *séance* or a lecture as regularly as she had eaten her supper. Her husband always had tickets for lectures; in moments of irritation at the want of a certain sequence in their career, she had remarked to him that it was the only thing he did have. The memory of all the winter nights they had tramped through the slush (the tickets, alas! were not car-tickets) to hear Mrs. Ada T. P. Foat discourse on the "Summer-land," came back to her with bitterness. . . . She had blinked and compromised and shuffled; she asked herself whether, after all, it was any more than natural that she should have wanted to help her husband, in those exciting days of his mediumship, when the table, sometimes, wouldn't rise from the ground, the sofa wouldn't float through the air, and the soft hand of a loved lost one was not so alert as it might have been to visit the circle. Mrs. Tarrant's hand was soft enough for the most supernatural effect, and she consoled her conscience on such occasions by reflecting that she ministered to a belief in immortality.

These are the guardians of the exquisite Andromeda, chained to the rock of the Philistines, about whom the battles rage in *The Bostonians*—that same Verena Tarrant who, in her fantastic costume, appears, springs up, before the astonished eyes of Basil Ransom, as if it were the necessity of her nature "to emit those charming notes of her voice, to stand in those free young attitudes, to shake her braided locks like a naiad rising from the waves, to please everyone who came near her, and to be happy that she pleased." James's young girls are always his happiest creations; it is as if they alone, of all his compatriots, filled him with frank satisfaction. Here again he resembles Turgenev, and like Turgenev, when he writes of them, he abandons his irony. Glance at this first sketch of Isabel Archer. A dozen words are enough to engage our affection; we are prepared to follow her, if the author wills it, through ten volumes, and we are aware from the first sentence that her destiny is not to be a happy one.

Her thoughts were a tangle of vague outlines, which had never been corrected by the judgment of people who seemed to her to speak with authority. In matters of opinion she had had her own way, and it had led her into a thousand ridiculous zigzags. Every now and then she found out she was wrong, and then she treated herself to a week of passionate humility. After this she held her head higher than ever again; for it was of no use, she had an unquenchable desire to think well of herself. She had a theory that it was only on this condition that life was worth living; that one should be one of the best, should be conscious of a fine organization (she could not help knowing her organization was fine), should move in a realm of light, of natural wisdom, of happy impulse, of inspiration gracefully chronic. . . . She spent half her time in thinking of beauty, and bravery, and magnanimity; she had a fixed determination to regard the world as a place of brightness, of free expansion, of irresistible action; she thought it would be detestable to be afraid or ashamed. . . . Altogether, with her meagre knowledge, her inflated ideals, her confidence at once innocent and dogmatic, her temper at once exacting and indulgent, her mixture of curiosity and fastidiousness, of vivacity and indifference, her desire to look very well and to be if possible even better; her determination to see, to try, to know; her combination of the delicate, desultory, flame-like spirit and the eager and personal young girl, she would be an easy victim of scientific criticism, if she were not intended to awaken on the reader's part an impulse more tender and more purely expectant.

Such is the population of this little world, this *piccolo mondo antico* that is yet so modern. And mingling with these Americans are the Europeans who cross their path, lightly sketched but closely observed, filling the middle distance. Lord Warburton, the Misses Molyneux, the dilapidated *cavaliere* in *Roderick Hudson,* Mr. Vetch, the old fiddler in *The Princess Casamassima,* M. Poupin, the exiled Communard, Miss Pynsent—how clearly they have been seen, how fairly judged! And who can forget Millicent Henning, daughter of the London streets, or the death of Hyacinth's mother in Millbank Prison? Such had been the result of James's first impressions in the London air, of the "assault," as he calls it somewhere, "directly made by the great city upon an imagination quick to react." He had seen England in relief against the world that he intimately knew. Faces at the window, figures in the doorway—the harvest of an ever-burning eye.

Yes, to this eye pensions and hotels and ocean liners and the streets and the theatres of the Old World have given up their secrets. "I have always thought the observant faculty a windy impostor," our author says in one of his early stories, "so long as it refuses to pocket pride and doff its bravery and crawl on all-fours, if need be, into the unillumined corners and crannies of life." And again, in his essay on Du Maurier: "There are certain pretensions [the thorough-going artist] can never take seriously; in the artist there is of necessity, as it appears to us, a touch of the democrat. . . . Du Maurier possesses in perfection the independence of the genuine artist in the presence of a hundred worldly superstitions and absurdities.'' James is to forget this truth as the years pass, but not for nothing has he prowled about in the days of his obscurity. His mind has retained its independence; he has, if not the universalized, at least the generalized consciousness of the authentic realist. Life judges itself through his perceptions, and behind what is he sees what ought to be. For he is by nature a social critic, a satirist, in the line of his adored Thackeray, Balzac and Turgenev.

A historian of manners, a critic of manners, a mind at home with itself, alert, witty, instructed, in its own familiar domain. Yes, and in the foreground of life, the ground of the typical, the general. Turgenev said of Flaubert's Monsieur Homais that the great strength of such a portrait consisted in its being at once an individual, of the most concrete sort, and a type. James creates these types again and again: they are not universal but they are national—there are scarcely half a dozen figures in American fiction to be placed beside them. Christopher Newman remains for all time the wistful American business man who spends his life hankering after the fine things he has missed. Daisy Miller's character, predicament, life, and death are the story of a whole phase of the social history of America. Dr. Sloper, that perfect embodiment of the respectability of old New York; Miss Birdseye, the symbol of the aftermath of the heroic age of New England; Mrs. Burrage, the eternal New York hostess; Gilbert Osmond, the

Italianate American—these are all veritable creations:
indeed one has only to recall Winterbourne, in *Daisy
Miller,* the American who has lived abroad so long that
he has ceased to understand the behavior of his fellow-
countrywoman, to perceive with what an unfailing re-
sourcefulness James infuses into the least of his characters the element of the typical. It goes without saying
that all this, together with the tenderness and the
benevolent humor that bathe the primitive Jamesian
scene, indicates the sort of understanding that is born
only of race. These novels are the work of a man who
was so sure of his world that he could play with it as
all the great novelists have played with their worlds.
The significant theme came to him with a natural inevitability, for he shared some of the deepest and most
characteristic desires of his compatriots. And this relation, as long as he maintained it, endowed him with the
notes of the great tellers of tales, the note of the satirist,
the note of the idyllist, the note of the tragedian.

And "how does he feel about life? What, in the last
analysis, is his philosophy? When vigorous writers have
reached maturity," James remarks in *Partial Portraits,*
"we are at liberty to look in their works for some expression of a total view of the world they have been so
actively observing." Nothing could be clearer than his
own view, the point, as it might be called, of these
gathered novels and tales. Mr. Hueffer says that
James's chief mission was to civilize America; and if by
civilizing one means the development of individuality,
the development of consciousness, one can hardly find a
happier phrase. He is the friend of all those who **are**

endeavoring to clarify their own minds, to know their own reasons, to discover their real natures, to make the most of their faculties, to escape from the lot of mere passive victims of fate. His tragedies are all the tragedies of *not knowing;* and those against whom he directs his shafts are the representatives and advocates of mass-opinion and of movements that mechanize the individual. He was the first novelist in the distinctively American line of our day: the first to challenge the herd-instinct, to reveal the inadequacy of our social life, to present the plight of the highly personalized human being in the primitive community. And James succeeds, where so many later novelists have failed, succeeds in presenting the struggle for the rights of personality—the central theme of all modern American fiction, because he is able to conceive personalities of transcendent value.

Yes, his own race, even his own soil—the soil to which he had remained for so long uneasily attached, the soil in which, in response to his own desire, he was brought back to be buried at last—was for James, in spite of all, the Sacred Fount. It was the spring of his own unconscious being; and the world to which it gave birth in his mind was a world that he saw with a level eye, as it was, as it should be, that he loved, hated, possessed, caressed, and judged. Judged it humanely, in the light of essential standards, of the "scale of mankind," in Dostoevsky's phrase, and by so doing created values for it. . . . As long as he retained a vital connection with it. But later? . . . "The world," says Mr. Lubbock, referring to his life in England, "is not used to such deference from a rare critical talent, and it certainly has much less respect for its own standards than Henry James had, or seemed to have. His respect was of course very freely mingled with irony, and yet it would be rash to say that his irony preponderated. He probably felt that this, in his condition, was a luxury which he could only afford within limits." That is discreetly put, but what it was to mean we can divine from one of his own early letters from London: "You will have read the second part [of *An International Episode*] by this time," he writes to his mother, "and I hope that you won't, like many of my friends here (as I partly know and partly suspect) take it ill of me as against my 'British entertainers.' It seems to me myself that I have been very delicate; but I shall keep off dangerous ground in future. It is an entirely new sensation for them (the people here) to be (at all delicately) *ironized* or satirized, from the American point of view, and they don't at all relish it." That is also discreetly put; nevertheless, it marks the beginning of the gradual metamorphosis of James's mind. He had seen life, in his own way, as all the great novelists have seen it, *sub specie æternitatis;* he was to see it henceforth, increasingly, *sub specie mundi*—for had he not subscribed, as only a probationer can subscribe, to the codes and scruples, the conventions and prejudices, the standards (held so lightly by everyone else) of the world he longed to possess? In adapting himself to this world he was to lose his instinctive judgment of men and things; and this explains his "virtuosity of vision," as Mr. Brownell describes it, the gradual decomposition, more and more marked the more his talent grew, of his sense of human values.

CHAPTER VI

THE WHEEL OF TIME

THE years had gone round and Henry James still found himself a stranger in a strange land. Long before—shortly after his arrival, indeed—he had met an observant German who had made his home in England. "I know nothing of the English," this man had remarked. "I have lived here too long—twenty years. The first year I really knew a great deal. But I have lost it!" Had not something of the same sort happened in James's case? He had submitted himself, as he said, without reserve, to the "Londonizing process," but had he become an "insider" in any other than "that limited sense" (to quote him again) "in which an American can ever do so"? His first impressions, his "recognitions," had been so poignant, so clear, so deep; he had felt as ·his Passionate Pilgrim had felt, that he had truly come into his own. How was it in reality? "I am getting to know English life better than American," he wrote in 1888, "and to understand the English character, or at least the mind, as well as if I had invented it." So he encouraged himself to believe—he was compelled to believe it. The fact remained, nevertheless, and it became more evident every day in his work, that he had failed to take root in the English world.

"With much that is common ground among educated people of our time and place he was never," says Mr. Lubbock, "really in touch. One has only to think of the part played, in the England he frequented, by school and college, by country-homes, by church and politics and professions, to understand how much of the ordinary consciousness was closed to him." Our first impressions of an alien scene are always so vivid that we feel we must know it better than those who have been born to it. In a sense, of course, we do; we realize it with a sudden intensity of which those to whom it belongs are incapable because they are so accustomed to it. But that is merely beginners' luck; when the novelty has passed away and we have lost our first sharp sensations, we perceive that the dwellers behind the threshold are truly in possession of the scene and that we are outsiders after all. And indeed with the English as he had found them James had nothing in common. "The love of the country, the love of action, the love of a harmless joke within the limits of due reverence, the love of sport, of horses and dogs, of family, of children, of horticulture." Thus, in his essay on Du Maurier, he sums up the tastes of his hosts—and which of these tastes had ever been shared by him? Common tastes, common instincts, are the basis of understanding; consequently, the longer he was to live, and the more intently he was to scan "the droll ambiguity of English relations, the fathomless depths" (as they appeared to him) "of English equivocation," the more he was to find himself in the position of the prince in *The Golden Bowl*. "He knew them, as was said, 'well'; he had lived with them, stayed with them, dined, hunted, shot, and done various other things with them; but the number of questions about them he couldn't have answered had much rather grown than shrunken, so that experience struck him for the most part as having left in him but one residual impression. They didn't like *les situations nettes,* that was all he was very sure of. . . .'' As for ''the inquiring mind, the result of its attention and its ingenuity, it had unluckily learned to know, was too often to be confronted with a mere dead wall, a lapse of logic, a confirmed bewilderment.''

Very little of all this—for reasons that we can well understand—appears in his correspondence of the time. ''The truth is,'' he writes in one of his letters, ''that the face of things here throws a sensitive American back on himself—back on his prejudices and national passions.'' And again: ''English life and the English character . . . offer themselves irresistibly as pin-cushions to criticism and irony.'' . . . ''Letter after letter,'' says Mr. Lubbock, ''is filled with caustic reflections on the minds and manners of the English.'' Most of these letters have evidently been suppressed, but we have only to turn to *The Tragic Muse,* James's one long attempt to picture English life realistically, to see how little sympathy he had with the people among whom he was thrown. The characters in *The Tragic Muse* are all measured by one criterion—are they ''on the side of art,'' are they ''in favor of art'' ? Those that are not—and they are the typically English characters—are pictured with a cold hostility that can only have been the result of a settled misunderstanding. . . . Ah, those high executive women,

those mothers of children, those consorts of officials,
those dispensers of hospitality! And those shooting,
riding, golfing, dining men! And politics, politics, politics all day long! The way they dropped that vague,
conventional, dry little "Oh!" settled any other question in the shortest order. They might go the length of
discussing for twenty minutes the relative charms of
Mr. Alma-Tadema and Lord Leighton, but the real point
remained outside their minds; after a little gentle worry-
ing they would give it up, and the conversation would
return to public affairs. There was "humbug and im-
becility" and there was "serious work"; there were
gentlemen, and there were "daubers" and the "des-
perately refined." The cold impatience of the Olympian eye would descend like a guillotine on one's emerging fancies. . . .

Yes, he was a stranger in a strange land. We are
obliged to go forward to find direct evidences of the
tenuity of his relation to English life; but Mr. Walpole
tells the whole story in his observation that James was
"American to the last in his attitude to Europe—quite
unconsciously using his notebooks as though he might be
called back to his country at any moment." In the light
of this remark, in the light of Mr. Gosse's recollection
that "he continued to be looked upon as a foreigner in
London," we are able to give due weight to the natural
complaint that recurs in his earlier letters: "I am still
completely an outsider here. . . . I have formed no inti-
macies—not even any close acquaintances. I incline to
believe that I have passed the age when one forms
friendships; or that everyone else has. I have seen and

talked a little with a considerable number of people, but I have become familiar with almost none." By giving due weight to these statements I mean that one easily reconciles them with Mr. Lubbock's affirmation that the "interested but slightly rebellious immigrant" had become with time the "old-established colonist"; for a colonist remains a colonist, and James was essentially, as Mr. Gosse says, a "homeless man."

This is the fact that must be borne in mind as we consider the main incidents of his middle years. Chief among these were his temporary abandonment of the novel and his efforts to find a foothold in the theatre. *"The Tragic Muse,"* he wrote to his brother in 1890, "is to be my last long novel. For the rest of my life I hope to do lots of short things with irresponsible spaces between." And again, to Howells: "I shall never again write a *long* novel, but I hope to write six immortal short ones." Along with this we find him remarking: "My books don't sell, and it looks as if my plays might. Therefore I am going with a brazen front to write half a dozen." In point of fact, nine years passed between the publication of *The Tragic Muse* and that of *The Awkward Age,* the first long novel in his "later manner," and for the greater part of this time he addressed himself with desperate zeal to the theatre. His motives in doing so have never been satisfactorily explained: it may be doubted, indeed, whether he himself was ever really aware of them.

There is no doubt, in the first place, that he was, in a sense, naturally drawn to the theatre. As a child, "I thought, I lisped, at any rate I composed, in scenes," he says in his reminiscences; and how genuine this interest was we can see as well from the vividness of his early recollections of the New York stage as from that of his impressions of the French stage in *The Tragic Muse*. Moreover, he was fascinated by what he called the "passionate economy" of playwriting. We have only to glance at the following passage from *Nona Vincent*, one of the stories which he wrote while he was in the midst of his dramatic fever, to see how keenly he felt this: "The scenic idea" (the young playwright is conceived as thinking) "was magnificent when once you had embraced it—the dramatic form had a purity which made some others look ingloriously rough. It had the high dignity of the exact sciences, it was mathematical and architectural. It was full of the refreshment of calculation and construction, the incorruptibility of line and law. It was bare, but it was erect; it was poor, but it was noble. . . . There was a fearful amount of concession in it, but what you kept had a rare intensity. You were perpetually throwing over the cargo to save the ship, but what a motion you gave her when you made her ride the waves—a motion as rhythmic as the dance of a goddess!" There we have, better expressed than anywhere else, the mood in which James was to return to his fiction, and we can see from his letters of the time that he had half persuaded himself that his true *métier* was the drama. "It has long been my most earnest and definite intention to commence at playwriting as soon as I can," he had written to his brother as far back as 1878; and this was the mood that crystallized at the beginning of the 'nineties. "I feel at last," he wrote, "as if I had found my *real* form, which I am capable of carrying far, and for which the pale little art of fiction, as I have practised it, has been, for me, but a limited and restricted substitute. The strange thing is that I always, universally, knew *this* was my more characteristic form, but was kept away from it by a half-modest, half-exaggerated sense of the difficulty (that is, I mean the practical odiousness) of the conditions."

He was naturally drawn to the theatre, then: of this we can have no doubt. We can only object that it would be rather singular for a born playwright to wait until he was nearly fifty before so much as attempting to write a play. Moreover, we have Mr. Gosse's word for the fact that his theatrical mania—for it seems to have been nothing less—passed away instantly after the fiasco of *Guy Domville:* he slept well that night, says Mr. Gosse, awakened calm the next morning and began to talk of his novels again, like a man who had returned to his right mind. All this indicates that the effort had been quite unnatural to him and that he was really relieved by the final demonstration of his failure; and would he, for that matter, have addressed his plays with such "extreme," such "extravagant deference to a theatre, to a company" (to quote his own words) if his heart had really been in them? "The convenience the piece had to square with," he writes, apropos of *The Reprobate,* in the preface to *Theatricals: Second Series,* "was the idea of a short comedy, the broader the better, thoroughly simple, intensely 'pleasant,' affording a liberal chance to a young sympathetic comedian, calling for as little acting as possible besides, skirting the fairy-tale, straining any and every point for that agreeable falsity, entailing no expense in mounting, and supremely susceptible of being played to audiences unaccustomed to beat about the bush for their amusement—audiences, to be perfectly honest, in country towns." And he adds that he was quite willing to provide the play with the "time-honored bread-sauce of the happy ending." Never, surely, has a writer exhibited a more complete "mush of concession," in Emerson's phrase, than that. Was there anything James would not have done to win success in the theatre?

Mr. Arnold Bennett, commenting on this episode, describes it as "pretty bad." It is "strange," he says, "how one artist may steal a horse while another may not look over a hedge." He adds: "Having failed to make money out of plays—and not, according to his own account, having failed to write a good play, James abandoned the drama. This also I think was pretty bad"; and indeed nothing could appear more anomalous than this lacuna, this yawning gulf, in a career that was otherwise so scrupulous. To all appearance James had simply suspended the operation of his literary sense; for five years he seemed to be living the life of an ordinary scenario-writer, with nothing but the difficulty of the undertaking to guarantee (as he put it) his intellectual self-respect; he swept aside all the arguments of his friends and devoted himself wholly, in Mr. Gosse's phrase, "to the infatuation of his sterile task"—and this at an age when most authors are in the fullest possession of their powers. But Henry James was not as others are, nor were his circumstances comparable with those of anyone else; and we should be greatly mistaken if we accepted any of the facts of his life at their face value. At this point, indeed, we cannot examine his motives too closely.

"My books don't sell," he wrote, "and it looks as if my plays might." And again, to his brother, after his failure: "The money disappointment is of course keen —as it was wholly for money I adventured." The fact was that while his American and "international" novels had had, if not a great, at least a considerable popular vogue, his subsequent work had been received with what appeared to be a steadily increasing indifference. Mr. Lubbock, however, deprecates his "belittling of his own motives," and one cannot but agree with him that "it seems impossible to take this language quite seriously." "For a man of letters with moderate tastes and no family," says Mr. Lubbock, "Henry James's circumstances were more than easy, even if his writings should earn him nothing at all; and he had no reason to doubt that his future was sufficiently assured." This point seems so well taken that we gladly follow Mr. Lubbock's further observations. "The sense of solitude that began to weigh upon him was perhaps more a matter of temperament than of fact; it never for a moment meant that he had lost faith in himself and his powers, but there mingled with it his inveterate habit of forecasting the future in the most ominous light. As he looked forward, he saw the undoubted decline of his popularity carrying him further and further away from recognition and its rewards; and the prospect, once the thought of it had taken root in his imagination, distressed and dismayed him. All would be righted, he felt, by the successful conquest of the theatre; there lay the way, not only to solid gains, but to the reassurance of vaguer, less formulated anxieties.''

The reassurance of vaguer, less formulated anxieties! Vague they must have been, at times—there were times and times, no doubt; unformulated always. But what were they? Was it not one of the consequences of his position that he was obliged to maintain the appearance of success? Like Rowland Mallet, in the first place, he had come to Europe on the tacit understanding that he was to do ''something handsome''; and who can forget the jeers and sneers which, a generation ago, attended every step of the way of the American for whom his own country was not ''good enough''? We can guess the effect upon James's pride of such an attitude as that which Colonel Higginson expressed when, in reply to someone's remark that our author was a cosmopolitan, he observed, ''Hardly, for a cosmopolitan is at home even in his own country!'' We have only to glance indeed at the caricatures of the illustrious expatriate that appeared in the American papers of the 'eighties and 'nineties to realize the extent to which he must have been stimulated to achieve the sort of success that would be understood by his distant countrymen. All this helps to explain the alarm that overtook him as he saw himself dropping into a relative obscurity; but there was another consideration that must have weighed upon him still more heavily, one that touched not merely his pride but the very foundation of his literary existence. In *The Siege of London* the young American Waterville remarks that while English society is always looking out for amusement its transactions are "conducted on a cash basis." That you have to pay for your footing in the great world is a truism to which James's characters have a significant way of referring; and as for James himself, does not Mr. Gosse marvel that one who had had so little to give as he should have been received so cordially at the outset? It was only as a celebrity, as a lion —was it not?—that he had any secure position in society; and now he had come to depend for his material on the hospitality of the very people whose requirements he had been less and less able to meet. The brilliant young American author had been a nine days' wonder; the nondescript Anglo-American with a waning reputation was in a different case. To keep open his one remaining avenue into life, to maintain his contact with the world that he had chosen, the only world that was left to him, he was compelled at all costs to retrieve his diminishing prestige.

Thus, as we see, it was nothing less than the instinct of self-preservation that drove him into the theatre. He had no choice but to "throw over the cargo to save the ship" (to quote his own phrase) ; for how could he hope to be able to write either novels or plays if he was to lose his access to the life that he had pledged himself to master? No wonder he was fairly "storm-ridden with emotion," as Mr. Gosse puts it, before the fatal night of *Guy Domville*. But there were other anxieties, still vaguer, still less formulated than these, perhaps, however closely connected with them, that filled his mind; and here we must return to the point with which I opened this chapter. He had remained a "foreigner" in England, he had remained a visitor, he had remained, as he said, a "mere paying guest in the house"; and the implications of this fact had gradually dawned upon him.

Did he know this English world? . . . It has been supposed by certain critics that James surrendered of his own will, at this turning-point in his life, the traditional novelist's rôle of a "secretary of society," that he more or less deliberately excluded nature "as seen" from his later work, that he voluntarily underwent a development comparable with that of certain contemporary painters who have withdrawn wholly into themselves and relinquished the representation of objects in the interests of abstract design. In point of fact, however, he clung to the literary habits and convictions of his youth. "I missed the *visible* in them," he writes to Stevenson in 1891, apropos of the opening chapters of some unnamed work of the latter, "I mean as regards people, things, objects, faces, bodies, costumes, features, gestures, manners. . . . No theory is kind to us that cheats us of *seeing*." He admires Balzac for being, precisely, "the patient historian," "the living painter of his living time," adding, in an essay written in 1892, "It is his assimilation of things and things that leaves his general image still coherent and erect." And he states his own constant purpose in another letter to Stevenson (1888): "I want to leave a multitude of pictures of my time . . . so that the number may constitute a total having a certain value as observation and testimony." His convictions thus remained unchanged, and so did his habits. "The great thing," he wrote to his brother, "is to be saturated with something—that is, in one way or another, with life; and I chose the form of my saturation"; and I have referred to Mr. Walpole's statement that he quite unconsciously used his notebooks to the last. In short, he never abandoned the conception of his art with which he had begun his career; moreover, he pursued with instinctive pertinacity the conditions that were favorable to it. "He was insatiable," says Mr. Lubbock, "for anything that others could give him from their personal lives. Whatever he could seize in this way was food for his own ruminating fancy; he welcomed any grain of reality, any speck of significance around which his imagination could pile its rings. It was very noticeable how promptly and eagerly he would reach out to such things, as they floated by in talk."

But what does it mean, this ravenous avidity, this unquenchable curiosity?—for Mr. Gosse also speaks of his having "demanded revelations, confidences, guesses." Does it suggest that he understood the world he was dealing with, that he was at home in it, that he had mastered it? "The great thing is to be saturated with something . . . and I chose the form of my saturation." He had chosen it: had he achieved it? Could he even believe that he had achieved it? "One thing only is clear," he wrote to Howells in 1890, "that henceforth I must do, or half do, England in fiction—as the place I see most today, and, in a sort of way, know best. I have at last more acquired notions of it, on the whole, than of any other world, and it will serve as well as any other. It has been growing distincter that America fades from me, and as she never trusted me at best, I can trust *her,* for effect, no longer." The last phrase we can disregard; its self-defensive note is self-explanatory. But we cannot disregard the preceding phrases. He had lost America, but he was far from feeling that he had gained any other world. An England that he was to "half do," an England that he knew "in a sort of way," an England about which he had "acquired notions" and which would "serve as well" as any other country, was not an England that he had conquered.

It is easier to understand now the resolution with which he brought his first phase to a close. "I shall never again write a *long* novel. . . . I am busy with the short—I have forsworn the long." Could he have expressed more unmistakably the consciousness that his English saturation had been abortive? In point of fact, *The Awkward Age* was his one subsequent experiment with a large, entirely English canvas. In the longer novels of his later period he returned to the "international" scene of his youth—the scene he had at first abandoned so reluctantly. Why had he "continued to write about Americans in Europe long after their common motive and their individual adventures had ceased to excite his wonder or his sympathy"? Miss Rebecca West, who asks this latter question, considers that James was the victim of a certain delusion about his art—in believing, that is, "that if one *knew* a subject one could write about it." That is a mistake; he was not deluded. He was not convinced that if one knew a subject one could write about it; he was convinced merely—it was of the essence of his belief as a realist, as a historian—that one couldn't write if one didn't know. "The effort of the novelist is to know," he was observing at this very moment in *Partial Portraits;* and "the only reason for the existence of a novel is that it does attempt to represent life." It was natural, therefore, that he should have been so cautious in surrendering his American world, that he should have clung to it until, as he said, it had "faded" from his mind; and it was very natural that, having at last undertaken to portray English manners on a similar scale, he should so soon have abandoned the attempt. In *The Princess Casamassima* he had "produced a picture gallery," as Miss Rebecca West says, "when he had intended a grave study of social differences." The book is full of enchanting episodes, but they remain "disconcertingly mere portals"; and what is *The Tragic Muse* but a single prodigious portal through which we never pass? It was projected as a "purely English" novel, as *The Princess Casamassima* was not, and it cost its author "long and patient and careful trouble," as he wrote, leaving his mind a "muddled, wearied blank." How little his knowledge of England had prompted him, how far from spontaneous the undertaking was, we can judge from this remark. It is a sufficient comment on the "Englishness" of *The Tragic Muse* that the scene of the novel is laid as much as possible in Paris and that the two most memorable characters are a Jewish actress and a young man whose home is in "Samarcand."

Such were the circumstances in which James concluded his first phase. He decided, Miss West says, to let his art "just beautifully soar." . . . "I'm destructively not national," she represents him as thinking; "my mind is engraved with the sights and social customs of half-a-dozen countries, and with the deep traditions of not one, and how can I deal deeply with the conduct of a people when I haven't a notion of the quality or quantity of the traditions which are, after all, its mainspring?" He was to soar indeed, but it cannot be said that he quitted the earth voluntarily. If he had achieved his English "saturation," if he had ceased to desire it, if he had ceased to feel that it was indeed the "great thing," we should not have found him in 1903 commenting on his "thin, starved, lonely, defeated, beaten prospect" and craving for the "vivid and solid *material*" which he felt that a return to his own country might give him. If he had ceased to desire it, he would never have been so conscious of the possession of it by others: he would never have felt that it was "mainly his saturation" that made Gissing interesting, he would never have been obliged to pay homage to Messrs. Wells and Bennett because they were so "enviably and potently" the masters of the "documented or saturated state." Saturation, the condition of being adequately steeped in one's material, of "knowing," as he put it, what we are "talking about," this, the merest matter of course with other writers, remained for James to the last a value of the first rank—a fact we have only to scrutinize in order to understand the vague panic into which he fell in the early 'nineties. It explains his

abandonment of the "long"; it explains his recoil to the
"short." It explains a further aspect of his effort as a
playwright.

As we shall see, all his later novels, even the longest,
were, essentially, "short." Does he not confess (1902)
to Howells that *The Sacred Fount*, "like *The Spoils of
Poynton, What Maisie Knew, The Turn of the Screw*,
and various others," was "conceived only as the 'short
story,'" was "planned . . . as a story of the '8 to 10
thousand words'" and then *"grew* by a rank force of
its own into something of which the idea had, modestly,
never been to be a book"? *"Given the tenuity of the
idea,"* he says, "the larger quantity of treatment hadn't
been aimed at. I remember how I would have 'chucked'
The Sacred Fount at the 15th thousand word, if in the
first place I could have afforded to 'waste' 15,000, and
if in the second I were not always ridden by a superstitious terror of not finishing, for finishing's and for the
precedent's sake, what I have begun." From this we
can judge how far any of the novels in question were, in
the form in which we have them, the fruit of an artistic
impulse that was at once spontaneous and sustained; and
do we not even find him frankly referring in his letters
to the "long-windedness" of *The Wings of the Dove*, to
the "vague verbosity" of *The Golden Bowl?* These later
novels are all—given in each case the tenuity of the idea
—stories of the "8 to 10 thousand words," blown out to
the dimensions of novels thanks to a method of which
James was to discover gradually the secret; consequently, to return to his plays, we can understand not
only why he wrote them but why, in spite of all his

protestations of a merely commercial motive, he wrote them with a good conscience. Granting that he had lost the immediate sense of life and character, that America had faded from his mind and that he knew he could never write of English manners with the intimacy and freedom which his conception of the novelist's task necessitated, the theatre was a natural resource. For there the plot would serve to take the place of everything.

Can we doubt that this was at the back of James's mind? "I find the *form* opens out before me," he writes to Stevenson, "as if there were a kingdom to conquer." Here he surmised but the truth, for the scheme of his later novels is essentially dramatic. His playwriting had been of the greatest advantage to him: it had given him a method that enabled him to carry on. But would he have required this form, would he have turned to it with such avidity, if the feeling for form had not supplanted in his mind the feeling for character? In the preface to *The Portrait of a Lady* he says that when he wrote the book he had scarcely been able to think of "any situation that didn't depend for its interest on the nature of the persons situated." He had begun with the "person" in those days, begun as Turgenev had begun, as later he was to begin with the "predicament"; and there we have the great distinction between primary and secondary fiction. Well, the theatre had taught him how to deal with "predicaments"—and had he not been attracted to it for still another reason? Mr. Lubbock remarks that he "could not have been so eloquent in his denunciation of all theatrical conditions, the 'saw-dust and orange-peel' of the trade, if he had not been enjoyably stimulated by them.'' When we consider how eager he was, a few years later, for the ''shocks'' of his own country, we find no difficulty in understanding this. Did he not feel, did he not perceive that he was drifting very far from the world of ''reality,'' from the common earth to which, to renew his strength, the artist, like Antæus, must ever return? ''He will find in you both,'' William James wrote in 1897 to two of his nieces who were on their way to London, ''he will find in you both . . . that direct swoop at the vital facts of human character from which I am sure he has been weaned for fifteen years at least. And I am sure it will rejuvenate him again.'' Was William James mistaken? Was Henry James unaware of the void towards which he was floating? We cannot believe it; and, disbelieving it, we cannot but think that the theatre seemed to offer him an avenue, a sanctioned, professional avenue, back to the general world of men and things. ''The vital facts of human character from which I am sure he has been weaned for fifteen years at least.'' Had he not, in his failure to come to grips with English life, fallen further and further away from the clutch of life itself? ''Persons'' had all but ceased to exist for him, and ''predicaments'' had taken their place; and during the transformation he had had to stoop to conquer. . . . Yes, he had stooped, he had bent for a while. But who could ever say that he had broken?

CHAPTER VII

THE FIGURE IN THE CARPET

BROKEN? Hardly! On the contrary, he had emerged with a new ambition. In abandoning the theatre, "in abandoning," as Mr. Gosse puts it, "the more popular and conventional method of composition, he aimed at nothing less than a revolution in the art of the novelist." He had lost something, but he had also found something. And what he had found was to fortify him through all the years to come.

He had lost something. It was not merely the following of the public. He had lost the basis of a novelist's life as he had once conceived it: a firm knowledge of the phenomenal world, a living sense of objective reality. Saturation and all it implies, everything of which he had written as giving the art of fiction "its large, free character of an immense and exquisite correspondence with life," as preserving it from "the hapless little rôle of being an artificial, ingenious thing" —this had slipped from his grasp. "The form," he had said, "is to be appreciated after the fact"; and ah, he had tried for the fact! He had tried for "the impression of life itself, and not of an arrangement, a réchauffé of life"—tried for the impression, tried for the life that germinates the impression. It was not his fault if he had been reduced to "the grain of suggestion, the tiny air-blown particle," to subjects that seemed to invite not so much the opera-glass as the microscope. It was simply that England was impenetrable. The harder he had pressed, the less it had yielded; and he had finally, luckily, happily raised the siege.

He had raised the siege, the siege of London—but never the siege of the Muse! If he still continued to take notes it was mainly from force of habit: he had lost the world, but he had found—what *hadn't* he found! English society had cut him "in two," as it cut Prince Amerigo: it had "fostered in him the determined need, while apparently all participant, of returning upon himself, of backing noiselessly in, far in again, and rejoining there, as it were, that part of his mind that was not engaged at the front. His body had been constantly engaged at the front, in bridge-playing, breakfasting, lunching, tea-drinking, dining; but he had reminded himself, in his relations with all these things, of a man possessed of a shining star, a decoration, an order of some sort which he kept concealed in his pocket." In was the shining star of his own private subtlety, and nothing in the world could ever deprive him of that.

Nor was this all. His whole consciousness had ached with a truth of an exquisite order, at the glow of which he had warmed himself. It had told him, with an hourly voice, that his life still had a meaning, a meaning that his sense was to drain even as thirsty lips, after the plough through the sands and the sight, afar, of the palm-cluster, might drink in at last the promised well in the desert; and how to bring it, by some brave, free lift, up to the height of his fortune was the idea with which, behind and beneath everything, he had been restlessly occupied. Yes, he had found something . . . the well in the desert . . . the figure in the carpet. And there was something else he had never lost. Powers and divinities: will and pride! What a life-preserver in the wildest waves was the perfect possession of a *métier!*

He had steeled himself; and now, through everything, his purpose held, his genius absolutely throve. Humility, labor, discipline! Not for nothing had he endured the dust and heat of the race. He had fulfilled his pledge, he had accepted his handicap, he had never deflected; he had taken up the gauntlet that Europe had flung at the feet of America and striven with faith and force. Yes, brazening it out was the secret of life, and he had waked and toiled while others slept; and the indifference of the English and the taunts of his own countrymen had only served to toughen his will the more. The pertinacity of his old Presbyterian grandfather at Albany, the gallant resolution of his father, toiling away amid the blank silence of the world, had passed into his own veins. It was as if they had imbued him for all time with the bravest confidence of calculation.

Yes, rigor and abstinence had fanned the fire in his brain. That strict regimen of a Puritan monk had quickened his mental machine. Moreover, to the re-sourcefulness of the old Yankee craftsman had been added the drill of France. He had scarcely written a page that was not the page of a scholar, and now at the end of time there was nothing he could not do. Esoteric things, personal mysteries, methods and secrets! If he had perceptions he had, like his own Miriam Rooth, traced them to their source; he could give an account of what he did; he could explain it, defend it, amplify it, fight for it. And all this was an intellectual joy to him, enabling him to abound and insist.

He had entered thus early on that period of life when, as Taine says, feeling vanishes before science and the mind especially delights in overcoming difficulties. "I find our art, all the while," he was to write betimes to Howells, "more difficult of practice, and want, with that, to do it in a more and more difficult way; it being really, at bottom, only difficulty that interests me." *Only* difficulty—and not the life he desired to represent? Only the way to do a thing that would make it undergo most doing? The day had not yet come perhaps when he was to forget the names of his characters, when he was to refer in his scenarios to "my first young man" and "my second young man," to "the Girl" and "Aurora What's-her-name," when he was to speak of the need of individuals simply of a particular size and weight; nevertheless, it is significant that the first novel in his later manner, *The Spoils of Poynton,* should have been, as he said, conceived as a story of "things." His people were to grow dimmer and dimmer, like the flame of a lamp in which the oil is exhausted; but he had found another object for his interest. He had found—*The Awkward Age* had proved it to him—that a novel might be "fundamentally organized."

That was the figure in the carpet, that was the joy of his soul; that was the very string his pearls were strung on. "By my little point I mean—what shall I call it?" says Hugh Vereker. "The particular thing I've written my books most *for*. Isn't there for every writer a particular thing of that sort, the thing that most makes him apply himself, the thing without the effort to achieve which he wouldn't write at all, the very passion of his passion, the part of the business in which, for him, the flame of art burns most intensely? Well, it's *that!*" It was the point Mr. Wells observed when he said that "James begins by taking it for granted that a novel is a work of art that must be judged by its oneness, judged first by its oneness"; and we have only to turn to our author's prefaces to perceive with what fervor he developed it. "A form all dramatic and scenic" was what he contemplated for *The Awkward Age*, "of presented episodes, architecturally combined and each making a piece of the building," and he began by drawing a diagram of "a circle consisting of a number of small rounds disposed at equal intervals about a central object"—the central object being his "situation." By such means he obtained his "rope, the rope of the direction and march of the subject, the action, pulled, like a taut cable between a steamer and a tug, from beginning to end." And he achieved his unity of effect by still another ingenious expedient. He defines this as his "preference for dealing with my subject-matter, for 'seeing' my story, through the opportunity and the sensibility of some more or less detached, some not strictly involved, though thoroughly initiated and intelligent, witness or reporter." In other words, the characters are presented to the reader as they are seen by one of them, the mind of the latter being alone presented directly.

Such was the general intention, the buried treasure, in the scheme of his books, upon which the creator of Hugh Vereker looked back with so much pride. He had reason to do so, for what craft, what cunning, what prodigies of deliberation, what arts of the chase had contributed to produce it! And this was only one of those innumerable "secrets of the kitchen" upon which he dwells in his later letters and essays. The "saturation and possession, the fact of the particular experience, the state and degree of acquaintance incurred," these elements, he says, constitute the circumstances of the interest of a novel: the interest itself lies where but in the "doing"? It lies, in short, not in the "matter" but in the "method"—and who had ever contrived such a method as his?

He had emerged as an impassioned geometer—or, shall we say, some vast arachnid of art, pouncing upon the tiny air-blown particle and wrapping it round and round. And now a new prodigy had appeared, a style, the style that was the man Henry James had become. He had eschewed the thin, the sharp, the meagre; he had desired the rich, the round, the resonant, and all these things had been added unto him; everything that he had thought and felt and tasted and touched, the fabrics upon which his eyes had feasted, the colors that he had loved, the soft sounds, the delicate scents, had left their stamp upon the house of his spirit. The house?—he had "thrown out extensions and protrusions, indulging even, all recklessly, in gables and pinnacles and battlements, things that had transformed the unpretending place into a veritable palace, an extravagant, bristling, flag-flying structure that had quite as much to do with the air as with the earth." His sense, like Adam Verver's, had been kept sharp, year after year, by the collation of types and signs, the comparison of fine object with fine object, of one degree of finish, of one form of the exquisite with another; and type and object and form had moulded his style. Metaphors bloomed there like tropical air-plants, throwing out branches and flowers; and every sound was muted and every motion vague.

For other things had passed into this style—the evasiveness, the hesitancy, the scrupulosity of an habitually embarrassed man. The caution, the ceremoniousness, the baffled curiosity, the nervousness and constant self-communion, the fear of committing himself—these traits of the self-conscious guest in the house where he had never been at home had fashioned with time the texture of his personality. They had infected the creatures of his fancy, they had fixed the character of his imaginative world; and behind his novels, those formidable projections of a geometrical intellect, were to be discerned now the confused reveries of an invalid child. For in his prolonged association with people who had merely glimmered for him, in the constant abrogation of his moral judgment, in these years of an enchanted exile in a museum-world—for what else had England ever been for him?—Henry James had reverted to a kind of childhood. Plots thronged through his mind, dim figures which, like his own Chad and Strether, "passed each other, in their deep immersion, with the round, impersonal eye of silent fish"; and with these figures, as with pawns or paper soldiers, he devised his labyrinthine games. What interested him was not the figures but their relations, the relations which alone make pawns significant.

Glance at these stories. Do they "correspond with life . . . life without rearrangement"? A man procures as a private preserve an altar in a Catholic church (*The Altar of the Dead*). A great author dies in a country-house because he is afraid to offend his hostess by going home (*The Death of the Lion*). A young man breaks his engagement to marry a girl he is in love with in order to devote his life to the discovery of the "intention" of a great author (*The Figure in the Carpet*). A young man who is described as a "pure, passionate, pledged Radical" agrees to act against his beliefs, stand as the Tory candidate and marry a girl he dislikes in order to keep his family estate (*Covering End*). The guests in a country-house devote themselves for three days to "nosing about for a relation that a lady has her reasons for keeping secret" (*The Sacred Fount*). A French countess who is presented to us as the type of the great lady loses her self-command when she is discovered in an equivocal situation, thrusts her daughter forward as a scapegoat and joins in a conspiracy not to hear the name of a certain undistinguished toilet-article (the Countess de Vionnet in *The Ambassadors*). A young man who is represented as "a gentleman, generally sound and generally pleasant," straightway appears without any adequate explanation as engaged in the most atrocious of conspiracies (Merton Densher in *The Wings of the Dove*). Two young men put away in a drawer without opening it a will which they have every right to open only to discuss for hours what the will probably contains (*The Ivory Tower*). A young man who is deeply in love abandons his betrothed because he is more deeply in love with a house he has inherited in London (*The Sense of the Past*). The reason we find these stories so oppressive is that they do not follow the lines of life. The people act out of character (Merton Densher), or in a fashion that belies their author's professions for them (the Countess de Vionnet), or in violation of the nature of things (the man who monopolizes the altar in the Catholic church) or as characters can only act with impunity to the author when they are presented ironically. It is intolerable to be asked to regard as "great" the Lion who is so afraid of his hostess, or as honorable the young politician who changes his party to save his house, or as worthy of our serious attention the lover who prefers his furniture to his mistress. Reset in the key of satire all these themes would be plausible; but James gathers grapes of thorns and figs of thistles.

No, the behavior of his characters bears no just relation to the motives that are imputed to them. They

are "great," they are "fine," they are "noble"—
and they surrender their lovers and their convictions for a piece of property. They are "eminent"—
and their sole passion is inquisitiveness. Magnificent
pretentions, petty performances!—the fruits of an irresponsible imagination, of a deranged sense of values, of
a mind working in the void, uncorrected by any clear
consciousness of human cause and effect. This is the
meaning of Mr. Richard Curle's remark that James had
become the "victim of his own personality." The general impression these writings give us—to quote a
phrase from *The Spectator*, is "that of a world in
which a brilliant conjuror manipulates puppets of his
own invention, not one in which the experience of real
life is transmuted in the crucible of creative genius."

The difference is precisely that which exists between
great acting and the cleverest ventriloquism. The actor
has realized his characters, he has lived them; the ven-
triloquist merely simulates their voices. With the latter
the sounds appear to come from some other source than
the speaker, but the speaker has never for a moment
projected himself into any other life than his own.
"We take for granted," James observes somewhere, "a
primary author, take him so much for granted that we
forget him in proportion as he works upon us." Yes,
we take the great novelists for granted, just as we take
the great actors. We forget Hardy, Dickens, Balzac,
Tolstoy; but that is because they have forgotten themselves; and they work upon us because of the intensity
with which they have shared our life. But when do
we ever forget the later James? We never pass be-

yond him, and we fall under his spell only to be unable
to return to ourselves. The great writers are transparent mediums, mirrors, shall we say, or "corridors,"
in Lamartine's phrase, through which life freely passes
back and forth between the mind and the world. The
later James stands between ourselves and life and creates
his illusion by benumbing our sense of human values.

We accept him therefore on his own terms or not at
all. On what other terms could we accept an art so
cerebral, an art in which all the cleverness of the
manipulation cannot conceal the poverty of the material? Mr. Wells's image of "Leviathan retrieving
pebbles," of the magnificent hippopotamus resolved
upon picking up a pea, is scarcely euphemistic; but
how else can we describe the monstrous disproportion
between the intellectual power at work in these novels
and our author's habit of "treating," as he calls it,
"an inch of canvas to an acre of embroidery"? If to
precipitate a world of meaning in a phrase, a paragraph, is an act of genius, what are we to say of the
reverse of the process? "What I want to do," James
remarks in the notes for *The Ivory Tower*, "is to get
out of *this* particular situation all it can give; what
it most gives being, to the last point, the dramatic
quality, intensity, force, current or whatever, of Gray's
apprehension of it." But the significance of a situation
depends wholly on the significance of the characters
that are involved in it, and Gray is too nebulous to
exist even as a ghost. "That which is firmly and
clearly imagined," says George Moore, "needs no psy-
chology." What other comment can one make on this

"quite incalculable tendency of a mere grain of subject-matter to expand and develop and cover the ground"?

We can only explain in a similar way those "ante-chambers" and "crooked corridors" that enabled James to evade the direct presentation of moments of emotional stress. "It's something like having saved his life," he remarks of some not yet imagined scene in one of his scenarios, "though that has a tiresome little old romantic and conventional note." But he could no longer conceive a major moment—he could no more do that than he could "go behind" his characters; and were not the laws, the prescriptions, the prohibitions that he invoked in behalf of his methods simply ration-alizations of his exiguities? To present a drama as it appears to the consciousness of a detached ob-server, "not otherwise going behind," is to create a very neat effect; but what does he mean when he says in one of his letters that "the promiscuous shiftings of standpoint and centre of Tolstoy and Balzac are the inevitable result of the quantity of presenting their genius launches them in"? Writers whose characters are vitally real to them and come to them with all their hidden thoughts and passionate moments will never be satisfied with a device that permits them to reveal only a facet of those characters—the insignificent facet that a mere observer sees. In his early books James had "gone behind," right and left, as he freely remarks. Was it not because he had known and felt, not merely watched from afar?

For the watcher is too apparent in these novels: we are always more conscious of him than of what he knows.

"The ingenious observer . . . our sharp spectator . . .
the acute observer . . . a supposititious spectator." I
am quoting a phrase that recurs through *The Awkward
Age,* and when are we allowed to forget this avid eye?
"Each of his later novels," says Mr. Littell, "is peopled
by protagonists who watch themselves and one another,
and by minor characters who watch the protagonists
sleeplessly. . . . Reading [*In the Cage*] was like watching Henry James watching through a knot-hole somebody who was watching somebody else through a knot-
hole." We remember Strether in Chad's rooms—daw-
dling, trifling, looking round, seeing, "sniffing"; and
the little telegraph-girl whose eyes devour every gesture of her patrons; and the scene in *The Aspern
Papers* in which the young editor steals into Miss
Bordereau's room just to see if he *can* move the lid of
the secretary. We remember that extraordinary theme
of *The Sacred Fount:*

"To nose about for a relation that a lady has her reasons
for keeping secret—"

"Is made not only quite inoffensive, I hold"—he immediately took me up—"but positively honorable, by being confined to psychologic evidence."

I wondered a little. "Honorable to whom?"

"Why, to the investigator. Resting on the kind of signs
that the game takes account of when fairly played—resting
on psychologic signs alone, it's a high application of intelligence. What's ignoble is the detective and the keyhole."

"I see," I after a moment admitted. "I did have, last night,
my scruples, but you warm me up."

And indeed the playing is fair enough, but what a game! Curiosity, as Mr. Brownell puts it, is "the one 'passion' celebrated with any ample cordiality by Mr. James."

Yes, he makes the very substance of this art out of his own failure to grasp the materials of it; for where the authentic novelist begins by possessing his people and then presents them in action, the James of these later books is reduced to presenting them merely in the act of discovering one another. "What is the leading motive of his people?" says Mr. Walkley. "Curiosity about other people's minds." It is the dramatization as it were of his own fixed attitude after all these baffled years in England, the attitude of what Hawthorne described as a "spiritualized Paul Pry"; and do we, in the end, know these people after volumes of exploration? A dim visual image—no heart, no mind, no vitals. No interests, no attributes, no activities, no race, no philosophy. No passions, ambitions, convictions: no local habitation—scarcely a name. They collect rarities, objects of beauty, objects of price, animate and inanimate; they become aware of other people as insubstantial as themselves; they drift in a confused limbo that knows no dimensions. They are made, as William James observed, "wholly out of impalpable materials, air, and the prismatic interferences of light, ingeniously focussed by mirrors upon empty space."

They are the products, in short, of prestidigitation, of the aesthetic chemistry of which their creator spoke; and was William James mistaken when he said that "the core of literature is solid"? "For gleams and

innuendoes and felicitous verbal insinuations," he wrote
to his brother, "you are unapproachable, but the bare
perfume of things will not support existence, and the
effect of solidity you reach is but perfume and simu-
lacrum." It is their interests, their attributes, their
passions, even their philosophy that create for us the
reality of the characters of fiction, and James had
strayed so far from his natural world that the tree of
knowledge had withered and died in his mind. Nor
was this all: he had lost not merely the power of instinctive perception, he had lost the artist's faculty of
disinterested judgment. When Mrs. Wharton taxed
him with no longer appreciating Flaubert, asking him
why Madame Bovary was not as good a subject as
Tolstoy's Anna Karenina, he replied, "Ah, but one
paints the fierce passions of a luxurious aristocracy, the
other deals with the petty miseries of a little *bourgeoise*
in a provincial town." He had cherished this delusion
from the first, but it had no more vitiated his early
criticism than it had prevented him from painting with
anxious delight the manners of his own countrymen.
The old magician who was baffled by *Ethan Frome* because, as he said, the characters of the story were
"such simple creatures as hardly to be worth the pains
the gifted writer had spent on them," who, for the same
reason, as we must suppose, found he could no longer
read *Washington Square* and for whom Ibsen was
scarcely anything but a "provincial of provincials . . .
ugly, common, hard, prosaic, bottomlessly bourgeois,"
had retained a craftsman's, but never, never an artist's
view of the world.

"What seems beautiful to me," Flaubert remarked in one of his early letters, "what I should like to write would be a book about nothing, a book without any external connection, which would support itself of itself by the internal force of its style, as the earth is held in the air without being supported; a book which would have hardly any subject—or at least in which the subject would be almost invisible." What remained with Flaubert a fancy had become with James the headstone of the corner. Yes, but those briefer pieces, *Crapy Cornelia, The Turn of the Screw, The Birthplace, The Beast in the Jungle,* those stories of the misunderstood author. They are beautiful indeed, beautiful in their soft splendor as clouds at sunset. Beautiful in their ambiguity, in their impalpability, they are the work, absolutely *sui generis,* of the minor artist for whom his own perplexities and the caprices of the imagination have taken the place of the knowledge and experience of life.

They are the "little tarts" to which James referred in a letter to one of his readers: "you shall have your little tarts"—a list of the stories he considered his best —"when you have eaten your beef and potatoes." He discriminated there between the major and the minor, and we cannot but accept the distinction. He had been the creator of an imaginary world, the historian of manners, the discoverer of human types; but those for whom formal significance, so essential in the plastic arts, is not the cardinal virtue of prose literature, for whom the world of fiction is to be judged by the vitality, the depth, and the variety of its content, will never be

satisfied with the novels of the later James—those ex-
halations of intellectual vapor, those nebulæ, shaped
like planets, that yet remain clouds of fiery mist. "It
is all very well," Mr. Ezra Pound remarks, "to say
that modern life is largely made up of velleities, at-
mospheres, timbres, nuances, etc., but if people really
spent so much time fussing, to the extent of the Jamesian
fuss, about such normal, trifling, age-old affairs as slight
inclinations to adultery, slight disinclinations to marry,
to refrain from marrying, etc., etc., life would scarcely
be worth the bother of keeping on with it." Who can
deny the justice of this?—and who can misread the
tragedy of Henry James? His tragedy was—Mr. Mid-
dleton Murry has expressed it—that he "yearned after
the fulness of European life which he could not join
again, and had to satisfy his impulse of asceticism in
the impassioned formalism of an art without content."

CHAPTER VIII

THE ALTAR OF THE DEAD

"JUST one year after my meeting with Alexandre Dumas I found myself at the residence of the late Viscountess Combermere, in Belgrave Square. It was on a Sunday evening, the 17th of April, 1870. As I sat there I could not help contrasting the company with the people I met at the residence of Dumas. There was still a glamour of art and romance in that company; in Belgrave Square I found myself among wealthy, titled people, among whom I could not discern so much as a glimmer of art, poetry, romance or intuition. London seemed to me a place whence the soul had departed; it was ripe for a reign of literary materialism which was to last for twenty years."

It scarcely needs to be said that James is not the author of this remarkable paragraph. Another pilgrim from America, no less enamoured than he of the charm of the Old World, had crossed the Atlantic at about the same moment and had also, after a year in Paris, found himself in the English capital. Was Mr. Francis Grierson just in his estimate of the scene that confronted him? Was it true that among these great ones of the British earth there was to be discerned no glimmer of art, poetry, romance, or intuition? Matthew Arnold had described them as barbarians, but that was only Arnold's little joke. They were really human, merely human—human, all-too-human.

Mr. Francis Grierson had perceived this at a glance. Not so Henry James. He had read his Thackeray not wisely but too well; he had not observed that little aside in which the author of *Vanity Fair* peeps down through the waves of Appearance and reveals for a moment the writhing and the twirling, diabolically hideous and slimy, of the tail of the monster Reality. He had taken Thackeray at his word: above the waterline everything had been proper, agreeable and decorous, and he had come to London with such a will to believe in the magnanimity of this dazzling British *monde* that he had at first seemed to discover in it the very counterpart of the world of which he had dreamed. And it was true that he had found on every side survivals of a more gracious time: great ladies who had known how to be old without being elderly and who had been accomplished without being clever, great ladies and great gentlemen, the pre-eminent, the historic gentlemen of whom he had read, of whom he had heard in a thousand connections, and who had been as witty and as kind as ever he had hoped they might be. Yes, he had found these Olympians whose names, whose every attribute, had reverberated as it were in his imagination with the intoxicating echoes of the noble, the commemorated, the literary past; and, having found them, he had seen everything that surrounded them in the light they seemed to shed. Moreover, and how natural it was, he had continued to read their qualities into the changing scene: he who had passed his childhood in

New York poring over Haydon's Memoirs and *Pendennis*, over *Punch* and Greville and *The Newcomes*, and who, by an inner necessity, had been compelled to find England as romantic as he desired it to be, could not easily surrender the vision and accept the reality. Nevertheless, as time had passed, he had become more and more aware that this world upon which he had built such hopes was not as he had imagined it. His eye had been bent upon the traces of the old order with a habit of anxiety that he could scarce have overstated—and what had become of the happy types *d'antan?* The "new plausibility" had taken the place of the "old sincerities"; the mellow had yielded to the garish, and the gracious had been succeeded by the smart. The "old England that an American loves" was rapidly passing into history. Nothing was left but little sorts of sets.

From the first there had been discordant notes in the harmony, and these notes had become more and more insistent. Disconcerting had been the moment when, years before, James had encountered face to face the poet he had earliest known and best loved. Tennyson had not been Tennysonian. Fine, fine, fine he had supposed the laureate would be, fine in the sense of that quality in the texture of his verse which had appealed all along by its most inward principle to his taste. He had never dreamed of a growling Tennyson, a swarthy, scraggy berserk, with a rustic accent, whose talk ran upon port wine and tobacco. . . . Tennyson had not been Tennysonian. . . . Had England proved to be altogether English? . . . Had not Europe itself positively ceased to be European? . . . One couldn't, to be sure, press the point too far. There had been his experience with Tennyson, for instance: once he had felt the old fond pitch drop of itself, an odd prosaic pleasantness had set itself straight up, substitutionally, over the whole ground—it had made his perceptive condition purely profane, reduced it somehow to having rather the excess of awkwardness than the excess of felicity to reckon with, but had yet enabled a compromise to work. And so it was with England in general. England for him could never lose its amenity, England for him could never cease to sing. Saxmundham, Romney Marsh, Yardley Chase—what names, and how they glowed and chimed again! And faces, gestures, voices, and the eternal mystery of the distinction of these people, and the greatness, yes, the greatness, incorruptible in the midst of its corruption, about which —with all sorts of unsatisfied curiosities and yearnings and imagings—he could never cease to hover. Could he ever lose that pang of interest, he who had not succeeded in plumbing these abysses, he who had never quite been able to penetrate into the Promised Land? But there are degrees of disillusionment, or rather one can be altogether disillusioned and still preserve, to the last intensity, one's amplest illusions; and there is no doubt that at fifty Henry James perceived that he had been in a sense a victim of that "immense fantastication" he had so enjoyed. He had been "a lover always of romantic phenomena and an inveterate seeker for them," and it was the romance—well, the palpable romance—that had somehow evaporated from the scene.

In 1899, after he had retired to Rye, he wrote to a friend: "I am only reacting, I suppose, against many, many long years of London, which have ended by giving me a deep sense of the quantity of 'cry' in all that life compared to the almost total absence of 'wool.' By which I mean, simply, that acquaintances and relations there have a way of seeming at last to end in smoke —while having consumed a great deal of fuel and taken a great deal of time." But long before this he had begun to complain of his predicament: more and more frequent, in his letters and stories, had been his protests against "the vast English Philistine mob," against "the gilded bondage of the country-house" and "that perfection of promptitude that makes the motions of the London mind so happy a mixture of those of the parrot and the sheep." In a letter to Norton in 1886 he expresses the same opinion of the English upper class as that which he had put into the mouth of the Princess Casamassima: "The condition of that body seems to me to be in many ways very much the same rotten and collapsible one as that of the French aristocracy before the revolution—minus cleverness and conversation; or perhaps it's more like the heavy, congested and depraved Roman world upon which the barbarians came down." He had found his fellow-writers in Paris "ignorant, corrupt and complacent"; and now, in England, these great people—they were doing, on every hand, things that one mustn't do if one is to remain great, if one is to retain the grand glamour of one's greatness. "Gouty, apoplectic, depraved, gorged and clogged with wealth and spoils, selfishness and scepti-

cism, bristling with every iniquity and every abuse"—
so they were, so they seemed, at least, in one's darker
moments. . . . "That was the real tragedy of the master's life," says Mr. Hueffer. "He had found English
people who were just people singularly nasty."

For behind this façade of an ageing man of the world
there was a child hidden, a Puritan child, and this child
had been shocked, perpetually shocked, it had been outraged and disappointed. What the man had accepted
with such avidity the child had never countenanced at
all; what the man had found the child had refused to
recognize. About 1890 there began to appear that series
of stories in the transparent depths of which one discerns
the troubled motions of their author's soul. *Broken
Wings, The Death of the Lion, The Velvet Glove*—how
often, in these brief and tenuous chronicles, he presents
the plight of the artist who has taken the fashionable
world at its word only to discover that it is just as
obtuse and materialistic and self-interested as that other
world upon which it looks down with such disdain.
"We can't afford the opulent. But it isn't only the
money they take," says Stuart Straith in *Broken Wings*.
"It's the imagination," says Mrs. Harvey. "As they
have none themselves——" "It's an article we have to
supply?" And all these writers and painters find themselves, like Neil Paraday, "badgered, bothered, over-
whelmed, on the pretext of being applauded," and
treated as mere instruments for the vanity of their
hostesses. There is John Berridge, the great novelist
in *The Velvet Glove*, who is so flattered because the
princess has sought him out and who finds that she

simply wants him to write a "lovely, friendly, irresistible log-rolling Preface" for a novel of her own. There is the "Lion," dying miserably at Prestidge, in the house from which he is afraid to extricate himself, while the other guests lose the manuscript of his new book and his hostess, who doesn't know the difference, devotes all her attention to Dora Forbes and Guy Walsingham, the authors of the latest shockers. There is Hugh Vereker, in *The Figure in the Carpet*, who is so "indispensable to Lady Jane" but whose young disciple steals down to the library at night and discovers that there is not a line of his writing in the house. "When," says James, in one of his prefaces, "when had I been, as a fellow-scribbler, closed to the general admonition of such adventures as poor Mrs. Harvey's, the elegant representative of literature at Mundham?—to such predicaments as Stuart Straith's, gallant victim of the same hospitality and with the same confirmed ache beneath his white waistcoat?" Decidedly, England had not lived up to his expectations.

Yes, he had been beguiled, he had been deluded. What did they care, these arrogant barbarians, with their gross tastes and their appetite for sensations, what did they care for the real thing, for the better sort, for the finer grain? It was a Philistine world, and the greatest were only the greatest Philistines. "No one has the faintest conception of what I'm trying for," says Neil Paraday in *The Death of the Lion*. "There's an idea in my work without which I wouldn't have given a straw for the whole job," says Hugh Vereker in *The Figure in the Carpet*. "It's the finest fullest intention of the lot, and

the application of it has been, I think, a triumph of
patience, of ingenuity. I ought to leave that to somebody
else to say, but that nobody does say it is precisely what
we're talking about." Or take the dying author in *The
Middle Years:* "It *is* glory—to have been tested," he
says to his one admirer, "to have had our little quality
and cast our little spell. The thing is to have made
somebody care. You happen to be crazy of course, but
that doesn't affect the law." Shall I mention *The Next
Time,* in which the exquisite genius Ralph Limbert tries
his best to write popular novels in order to make money
for his family and succeeds in producing each time just
one more hopelessly beautiful and utterly unsalable
work? Or *The Abasement of the Northmores,* in which
the real genius is never recognized, while his rival, who
deserves nothing, gets all the honors? Or *John
Delavoy,* in which the famous editor Mr. Beston refuses
to publish the beautiful tribute to the great artist who
has died and tries to worm out of his sister the vulgar
personal gossip that his readers want? James himself
tells us that the material for these portraits of misunderstood authors was drawn from the depths of his own
experience; and what a comment they are upon the else
unspoken bitterness of his own disenchantment! London, England, Europe, where he had supposed that the
great were always great, that the honorable were always
honored, that the fine was always perceived and the
noble invariably appreciated! Alas, for that superstitious valuation of the Old World against which he had
fought a losing battle! "Bottomless vulgarity"! It
had come to nothing less.

Is it necessary to labor the point? Is it necessary to remark that the virtually invariable theme of his later writings is the victimization of some innocent cat's-paw at the hands of conspirators or of a negligent, insensible, malevolent and callous world? The story of *The Other House* turns on the murder of a child. Fleda Vetch's life ends in tragedy because she is too fine for those among whom her lot is cast. The little girl in *What Maisie Knew* is as helpless as Nanda in *The Awkward Age*. Then there is *The Turn of the Screw* in which the author's intention was to give, as he says in one of his letters, "the impression of the communication to the children of the most infernal imaginable evil and danger"; and *The Golden Bowl,* with Maggie Verver deceived in her own household, and Milly Theale in *The Wings of the Dove,* victim of the basest plot that ever a mind conceived. It is true perhaps that in this world the "low sneaks" have it all their own way, true that the subtle are always the prey of the gross, that the pure in heart are always at the mercy of those that work iniquity. But why did the predicament of the innocent victim possess for James such an irresistible fascination? We shall never know, we can only surmise; we can only observe that the series of novels and stories of which I have spoken, those stories in which a child or a young girl is usually the victim and which seem to express James's final and settled view of life, immediately follow that other series of briefer pieces in which he presents the plight of the great author *incompris,* of the "poor sensitive gentleman"—"my attested predilection for poor sensitive gentlemen," he remarks in one of his

prefaces, "almost embarrasses me as I march!"—who is
"too fine for his rough fate." Had he not himself been
somehow deceived from the first, he who had grown up
with his dream of the Old World, who had accepted the
whole "European" dispensation with that extraordinary
American good faith, who had so diligently learned the
ropes—yes, to make himself worthy!—and who had
never been able to conceive of the American in Europe
in any light save that of a tragic futility? With what
humility he had espoused the great Matthew Arnold's
counsels of perfection, sought the centre, eschewed the
provincial, studied the urbane. He had toiled up the
rocky slope of the British Olympus, and he had arrived
at twilight and found the gods nodding on their dilapidated thrones. Ah, that wondrous fairy-tale of his
youth—the Europe of the American! It had flown away
as a dream, as a vision of the night.

"I *have* felt, for a long time past," he writes to
Howells in 1895, "that I have fallen upon evil days—
every sign or symbol of one's being in the least *wanted*,
anywhere or by anyone, having so utterly failed." The
feeling that he was "utterly out of it" oppressed him.
Editors neglected him, the public ignored him; he felt
as if "condemned to eternal silence." And now every
sort of doubt and misgiving had begun to assail him:
*The Altar of the Dead, The Great Good Place, Maud-
Evelyn, The Beast in the Jungle*, stories in which his
talent reached its clearest autumnal beauty, reveal to
us the perplexities, the regrets, the longings that hov-
ered over the threshold of his consciousness. "You
understand," he said to Mr. Hueffer, "I *wanted* to write

The Great Good Place and *The Altar of the Dead.* . . .
There are things one wants to write all one's life, but
one's artist's conscience prevents one. . . . And then
. . . perhaps one allows oneself.'' Ah, that Utopia of
material simplification! He seemed, in the endless press
and stress, to have lost possession of his soul, he seemed
to be surrounded only with the affairs of other people,
to be smothered in mere irrelevant importunity! And
the dead that were so quickly forgotten in London:
who cared for the dead, who cared for the finely living,
in this hurly-burly, this clamorous rout, this clumsy,
expensive, materialized, brutalized, snobbish British
world? Who remembered, lamented, perceived, discerned, cherished *anything?* Vulgarity reigned on the
house-tops, blown and red in the face.

Ah, these infatuated Americans! Wolcott Balestier,
for instance, dying of typhoid in his mouldy old chambers in Westminster—because he had loved their pic-
turesqueness. It was terrible to be so at the mercy of
the picturesque. And there was Whistler: he, too, had
been incomprehensible to the English, he had been vili-
fied, bespattered, maligned. It was not so easy, this
living between two worlds: one got nothing for one's
pains but neglect, insults, derision. One received no
recognition anywhere: what was worse, one lost touch
all round, one ceased to understand, one ceased to be
understood, one found oneself gradually encompassed
by an atmosphere that was somehow non-conductive.
Wasn't it true that the great writers had always stood
in some vital relation to their audience, that there was
a certain necessary give-and-take between a novelist and

his own people? It was all very well to talk about the rabble and their opinions, but it was another thing to be unable to speak a word of their language: had not even the contemptuous Flaubert been hurt, astonished, unsettled by the mingled indifference and hostility with which the public had received his *Education Sentimentale?* And Flaubert had had his friends, his fellow-craftsmen. For himself there had been . . . well, R. L. S., the sole and single Anglo-Saxon capable of perceiving how well one wrote. The others? For them art was pardonable only as long as it was bad.

Yes, he had been so utterly lonely here. What community was there, what *could* there be, between himself and these new English writers, these irreverent usurpers, these Coquecigrues, with their bad manners and their crazy desire to change things! These Butlers and Shaws, who had turned against everything that was lovely and of good report and did not stop even at fouling their own nests! Kipling, the infant monster, with his brass band, brawling about steam and patriotism. Havelock Ellis and his abhorrent "major topic." Wilde and Beardsley and their ignoble crew of British æsthetes, upstarts and vulgarians to a man, with their Frenchified patter and their extraordinarily base ideas. He had been driven to make common cause with the "Yellow Book"—up to a point. It had given him an outlet when outlets were few; it had permitted him a certain latitude in regard to the development of his stories; but how he had hated its horrid aspect and its company of cads! What did they know, any of these people, about the old gracious England that was tumbling—what did they care?—about their heads? And besides, they were not really artists, any of them, they were gamins with their tongues out. Had he, as a matter of fact, known *any* artists, R. L. S. aside, during all these English years? One's friends, of course—but seriously? One scanned in vain the boundless void, one scanned the desert sands. There was Fanny Kemble who had despised her art. There was Mrs. Ward—dear good lady, she had never understood a single word he had said! And Meredith. He had had with Meredith no sense of reciprocity: he had simply sat before him till the curtain fell and then come again when he felt he should find it up. R. L. S.—where *he* had been had descended an avalanche of ice.

At best he had lacked the time. Had any other novelist ever been obliged to fix his mind so undeviatingly upon the study of his chosen world? It had not been so simple—had it even been possible?—to master a world in which he had had no inherited property. How much he had had to give up for it! He had had to prune his life, to trim it of half the interests of the normal man. He had been obliged to surrender all sorts of things, the easy companionship of his fellow-workers—above all, perhaps, travel. How could he have afforded to dissipate his forces, to run the risk of confusing his impressions? He had seen from the first that only by virtually turning his back upon the rest of Europe could he hope to make himself at home in a single corner of it. France and Italy, for an occasional holiday or a season of work, France and Italy . . . he had not been able to stray for a moment from the

familiar highways of his youth. Had he not lived in
constant fear of watering too far his little acquired
stock, his accumulated capital of international items
and properties? Had he not always been in danger of
losing all that he had gained of England, England the
irreducible, the unconquerable? It had been a choice,
for him, of missing everything or going under; and had
he, in the end, really lived at all? That was the Beast
in the Jungle, the fate that he had been marked for:
he had been the man of his time, *the* man, to whom
nothing on earth was to have happened. It was as if
the train had fairly waited at the station for him, and
he had been too preoccupied to know it was there. And
now he heard its faint receding whistle miles and miles
down the line.

There was no doubt of it: he found himself astray
in the gloomy wood. Ghosts and echoes, memories and
sighs: in the absence from his life of such other elements, either new pleasures or new pains, as abound for
most people, it was as if the air had suddenly become
peopled with phantoms. Ah, the starved romance of
his days and that sense of being hollowed out within!
The great thing had always been to be saturated with
something—in one way or another with life; and his
own saturation had given out, had run short. He had
scarcely scraped the surface of Europe; he had been too
old to attach himself to another country. It was as if
he had not lain on the ground, not touched the ground,
for twenty years, as if he had been living in a balloon.
His real judgments about England he had scarcely been
able to utter to a single Briton of them all with the

faintest chance of being understood. Everything had
been corked up. He had had no one but Howells upon
whom to inflict these sordid groans.

Was Howells right, after all?—had it really been "too
much" for him over here? Howells himself had had
the advantage of breathing an air that had suited him
and nourished him, of sitting up to his neck amid the
sources of his inspiration. *He* had never had to prac-
tise these mean economies. His works had savored
strongly of his native soil, like those of all great novelists; and if he had not been great, well, that was another
matter. And hadn't America been really finer, that old
America of their youth, plainer, severer but lovelier in
its clear innocence, its spontaneity, its intellectual grace,
its Emersonian purity, ethereal as the day-spring, lovelier, more delicate, more essentially sympathetic than
this unconscionable old Europe? Why had he not been
able to fall in with it? Why had he quarreled with it?
"Indeed I know," says Mr. Hueffer, "that, towards the
end of his life, he came to think that the society of early,
self-conscious New England, with its circumscribed
horizon and want of exterior decoration or furnishings,
was a spiritually finer thing than the mannered Euro-
peanism that had so taken him to its bosom. . . . When
I first knew him you could have imagined no oak more
firmly planted in European soil. But, little by little,
when he talked about America there would come into his
tones a slight tremulousness that grew with the months.
. . . Occasionally he would burst out at me with furious
irritation if I ventured to have any opinions about the
United States. . . . I remember one occasion very

vividly—the place, beside one of the patches of thorn
on the Rye road, and his aspect, the brown face with the
dark eyes rolling in the whites, the compact, strong
figure, the stick raised so as to be dug violently into the
road. He had been talking two days before of the
provincialism of Washington in the '60's. He said that
when one descended the steps of the Capitol in those
days *on trebuchait sur des vaches*—one stumbled over
cows, as if on a village green. Two days later, I don't
know why, I happened to return to the subject of the
provincialism of Washington in the '60's. He stopped
as if I had hit him, and, with the coldly infuriated tone
of a country squire whose patriotism has been outraged,
exclaimed: 'Don't talk such damnable nonsense!' "
Had there not been something in America more important than misplaced cows?

His mind had begun to teem with old associations
. . . Lowell . . . Hawthorne. . . . Hawthorne, too, had
lived in a world of shadows and allegories; but his shadows had been so palpable and his allegories, after all,
so firm. And what had the old wooden houses signified,
the mud and the dust, the dead level of site and sentiment, the chill east wind, the chilliest of social atmos-
pheres? His spell had subsisted, and just as potently
as if Salem had been an earthly paradise. Was it
possible—could he himself have survived in America?
If he *had* stayed, if he *had* gone back, and if . . . What
mightn't he have done with people he would have really
understood, people he could have approached *en maître*,
whose thoughts would have been his thoughts, whose
feelings would have been his feelings, whose desires

would have been the desires of his own flesh and blood? If he hadn't had to be on the defensive as regards his opinions and enjoyments? If he had been able to live without pomp and circumstance to back him, without mystery and ceremony to protect him? If he had been able to read the universe into his own country as Balzac had read it into France? . . .

Well, his life had been conditioned and related and involved—it had been, so to say, fatalized . . . and yet. There was William, perpetually urging him to come home . . . if he wanted some "real, roomy, rustic happiness" . . . with a wood-pile as large as an ordinary house and a hearth four feet wide and the American sun flooding the floor . . . at Tamworth Iron Works. That was just it: Tamworth Iron Works. You could feel the rust on your fingers, and the weeds and the litter and the dilapidation—and the roominess, for that matter, and the rusticity, and the bare pine boards, and that everlasting, that absolutely empty, that positively terrifying forest, and the bouncing, bustling promiscuity of the whole business. One had to face facts. . . . And yet, when one *didn't* face facts, when one *didn't* come up to the surface and glare about but just drifted, allowed the stream to carry one along, down there, among the seaweed, where the light was so ambiguous, one saw, felt, heard—yes, one heard something, a knock, the knock of an old vagrant question. "A man always pays, in one way or another, for expatriation, for detachment from his plain primary heritage." Story had felt that; he had never failed of any plenitude in feeling it, in the fulness of time and on due occasion. How many others had felt it?—and what had he himself paid, paid for having sought his development even among the circumstances that had appeared not alone the only propitious but the only possible? It was truly as if the circumstances on which, to do this, he had turned his back had found an indirect way to be avenged for the discrimination.

One might certainly over-estimate the intensity with which James consciously entertained any such thoughts as these. At this very moment he was remarking, in a paper on Henry Harland, that the time had come for "looking more closely into the old notion that, to have a quality of his own, a writer must needs draw his sap from the soil of his origin." But how much of the will to believe in his own destiny, how much of the unconscious pragmatism which he said he had always practised, what an immense need of self-justification had obliterated from his sight the instinctive beliefs and desires and misgivings that carried on their drama in the depths of his soul! To accept his letters at their face value, his published statements, is to misconceive him entirely; or shall we say that he expressed the whole truth about himself in his casual correspondence and none at all in those more private passages from which his brother concluded that he felt his career was "going to seed"? There was truth in both sets of utterances— in those that expressed the self-confidence of the triumphant craftsman, the man who, as Mr. Lubbock says, "knew perfectly what he wished to do and knew that he could do it," and those others, few and shy and heavily censored, that conveyed his regrets and his fears;

and there is no doubt that, at the turn of the century, nothing occupied his mind more than the question whether he might not have survived more effectually in America. It had ceased to be a practical question, it had never ceased to be a real one. The publication, in 1897, of Maurice Barrès's *Les Déracinés* could never have supplied him, as Mr. Gosse says it did, with "an endless subject of talk and reflection" if he had ever satisfactorily settled the problem of his own deracination.

Nor is this the only evidence of the confused suspicions that the wheel of time had brought to the threshold of his consciousness. Why, in the American Letters which, in 1898, he contributed to *Literature,* did he illustrate his remark that "saturation is almost more important than talent" by adding: "The point I for the moment make is simply that in the American air I am nervous in general lest talent should wish to 'sail for Europe' "? Why did he write of Mrs. Wharton: "She *must* be tethered in native pastures, even if it reduces her to a back-yard in New York"—adding that this was the pure essence of his wisdom and experience? Why did he write to Mrs. Wharton herself: "Your only drawback is not having the homeliness and the inevitability and the happy limitation and the affluent poverty of a country of your own"? One recalls the advice which he gave his elder brother in regard to the bringing up of the latter's children: "What I most of all feel, and in the light of it conjure you to keep doing for them, is their being *à même* to contract local saturations and attachments in respect to their *own* great and glorious country, to learn, and strike roots into, its infinite beauty, as I suppose, and variety. . . . Its being that 'own' will double their *use* of it." And one observes, too, that about this time (shortly before he turned to the life of Story) he began *The Sense of the Past* which opens with the figure of Aurora Coyne, who has had " 'somewhere abroad' . . . an encounter, an adventure, an agitation" that has filled her with "rage or shame, leaving behind it a wound or a horror," who has come back to America to "take up definitely," as she says, "with my own country," who wants to be "an American, as other people are—well, whatever they are" and begs Ralph Pendrel to stay with her. "What I'm dying to see," she says, "is the best we can turn out quite by ourselves. My cold little theory is exactly indeed that it would be interesting to catch you—catch you young, as they say, since you *are* young—and put you through . . . I should see what it makes of a man." Can we doubt that James was asking there a question of his own, the question that had occupied him all his life long?

Now, at any rate, in the midst of his ruminations, there had gradually gathered in his mind a dimly formulated idea. To go back to America, to retrace the past, to see for himself, to recover on the spot some echo of ghostly footsteps, the sound as of taps on the window-pane heard in the glimmering dawn. . . . It was odd how romantic, in the evening of his days, his own country had become for him—romantic as Europe had been in the dreams of his earlier time. The European complexity had grown so usual and calculable, the old oracle sounded in his ears so enfeebled, shrunken, and spent: what might not America have in store for his relaxed curiosity, his limp imagination? It was rather terrifying: like Mrs. Gereth, he had lived for twenty years in such warm closeness with the beautiful that he could scarcely leave his house without peril of exposure. But he was hungry for material, for an "all-round renovation of his too monotonized grab-bag"; he needed shocks, and where could he look for them now, where could he look for his "one little ewe-lamb of possible exotic experience" if not in the land of the Vocalization, of the Shocks in General? . . . Such were the reasons that came to his lips as, more and more definitely, the project of a return to America took form in his mind: the writer had become aware of a supreme opportunity, the restless analyst, the seeker of romantic phenomena had caught the scent from afar. But who can tell what other thoughts had come to him on the breast of the river of time? What airs, what floating whispers, vague and forlorn? Ah, that old remembered breath of New England woods and New England waters . . . and the rustle, the smell of the October leaves in Washington Square, trodden by the feet of his childhood—the murmur of that other, the American, the prehistoric existence. And those long-forgotten walks with Howells round Fresh Pond, the problems, the questions, overlaid but never answered, the ghost of the self that he would, that he might have been. "I remember," says Mr. Hueffer, "once he went to see some friends off to New York from Tilbury Dock. He came back singularly excited, bringing out a great many unusually uncompleted sentences. He had gone over the liner: 'And once aboard the lugger. . . . And if . . . say a toothbrush . . . and circular notes . . . and something for the night. . . . And if. . . . By Jove, I might have . . .' All this with a sort of diffident shamefacedness. . . ."

Twenty, forty, sixty years. For even so had his father invoked the dividing sea.

CHAPTER IX

TERMINATIONS

HE had come back, back to England, back to Rye.
He had fairly staggered back—like the hero of
"Crapy Cornelia"—wounded, bleeding, blinded from
the riot of the raw. It had all been calculated to make
him crouch, for the rest of his life, as closely as possible,
to make him curl up forever in his little old-world
corner.

It had been, to be sure, a magnificent sally. Impressions! For twenty years they had not rained upon him,
from every tree, so thick and fast. His languor had
fallen from him as the tattered skin of some torpid
creature of the jungle reawakening to the spring.
Twenty years, thirty years: not since those first de-
licious months in London had he known such exhilara-
tion, had he experienced such a feeling of adventure, of
romance. Excited at every turn had been that desire
of the writer to linger where the breath of a subject
faintly stirring the air, reaches his vigilant sense. The
challenge to speculation had been fed by a thousand
sources. He had come back as a Goth from Rome positively gorged with spoils.

There was no doubt about the spoils. There was no

doubt about the crackling twigs—armfuls of them and
how they crackled!—that he had been able to pile up on
the altar of perception: it had been a game of feeding
the beautiful iridescent flame, ruddy and green and
gold, blue and pink and amber and silver, with anything
he could pick up, anything that would burn and flicker,
and he had scarcely been able to move for the brush that
clogged his feet. New York, Boston, Newport—Newport
where the small silver whistle of the past, with its
charming quaver of weak gayety, had quite played the
tune he asked of it up and down the tiny, sunny, empty
vistas; and poor dear queer flat comfortable Philadel-
phia, and Richmond with its invalid gentleness, its dim
smile of modesty, and sweet frustrated Florida, and
California with the wild flowers fairly raging with
radiance over the land. There had been harsh impressions and happy: the consummate monotonous common-
ness of the pushing Broadway crowd, moving in its dense
mass, with the confusion carried to chaos for any intelligence, a welter of objects and sounds, and the cherished
American vaguenesses, hailed again, the dear old name-
less, promiscuous lengths of woodside and waterside,
things to play on the chords of memory and association.
(Ah, that general iridescence, at Albany, in the New
Hampshire woods, of a past of Indian summers hanging
about mild ghosts half asleep, in hammocks, over still
milder novels!) And golden autumn days, with weather
like tinkling crystal and colors like molten jewels, and
winter days dazzling and bell-like in their frosty clear-
ness. It had been almost uncannily delightful and
sympathetic: what more could the revisited scene, what

more could any scene, have set rolling over the field of a prepared sensibility?

Yes, for the restless analyst, for the brooding analyst, it had served positively as a redemption. He had felt his relaxed curiosity revive, he had found his limp imagination once more on the stretch. What notes he had been able to store away, what happy phrases! And happiest of all, perhaps, had been the reassurance, the reassurance . . . he *had* wondered, but it was all right . . . he had *had* misgivings, but it *wasn't* the test of a great author that people bought one's books. Hadn't they gaped at him, in his native land, actually as the Red Indians had gaped at the first visiting white man? And there had been that other reassurance; he had had his doubts; but no, once and for all, he couldn't have survived, in any way that he would have wished to survive, in that air of unmitigated publicity, publicity as a condition, as a doom, from which there could be no appeal. He had taken pains not to see anything of the "littery" world, but hadn't he felt it, heard it, divined it? Hadn't he *read* the little tales, mostly by ladies, and about and for children, romping through the ruins of the language in the monthly magazines? And how plain was the evidence that there was, and had been these many years, no place in America for the American who "makes" too little for the castle and yet "minds" too much for the hustled herd? To make so much money that you wouldn't, that you didn't mind, didn't mind anything—that was obviously the main American formula. Not to have made the money would have been to forgo the castle, and how could one have made the

money without the magazines? It was a relief to see
it all so clearly.

He had been, for the rest, repelled—so amusedly, so
sadly—repelled, outraged, disillusioned. He had turned
his steps, for the pleasure of memory, to Fresh Pond,
dear to the muses of the prime, the Sunday afternoons
of spring, and had almost angrily missed, among the
ruins, the ruins of the "large extension," what he had
mainly gone back to recover—some echo of the dreams
of youth. He had looked in Boston for the accent, for
the ghosts of other days, and he had felt that half his
history had been amputated. In New York his birthplace had vanished: it was as if the bottom had fallen
out of his biography. There had been objects, signs,
notes in the scene, a little soiled and sordid now, that
had been there from far, far back, things he hadn't had
to wear a green shade to look at; and he had had quite
the sense for the moment of asking them, of imploring
them, to recognize *him*, to be for him things of his own
past. But in the end the revisiting spirit could but
muffle its head and turn away forever. The new land-
marks had crushed the old as violent children stamp on
snails and caterpillars; and everywhere, on all sides, the
gross alien was in serene and triumphant possession.
Ah, that air of hard prosperity, that ruthlessly
pushed-up and promoted look worn by men, women, and
children alike! And the bigness and bravery and insolence of everything that rushed and shrieked! And
the utter absence of the *interior*, the proscription of privacy, and the drummer on the train, and the lone breakfasting child in the hotel, the little pale, carnivor-

ous, coffee-drinking ogre or ogress, who prowled down in advance of its elders, engaged a table—dread vision! —and had the run of the bill of fare. New York—ah, that awful "step lively"!—New York was practically a huge, continuous fifty-floored conspiracy against the very idea of the ancient graces. And the ubiquitous elevator, the abject collective consciousness of being herded and driven, of being pushed and pressed in, with something that one's shoulders and one's heels had to dodge at one's peril, something that slid or slammed or banged, operating, in one's rear, as ruthlessly as the guillotine. Even worse, perhaps, had been the perpetual effort to "do justice" to what he hadn't liked.

He had experienced, above everything, a sense of absolute dispossession. It had become clear to him, the shuddering pilgrim, that he could indeed return again (could be carried back on a stretcher) to die—but never, never to live. He had felt in America nothing but a transcendent homesickness for England; in the heart of golden orange-groves he had yearned for the shade of the old Lamb House mulberry-tree; he had been sustained indeed at every moment by a sort of private reference to the fact that he *had* a tight anchorage, a definite little downward burrow in the ancient world—a secret consciousness that he had chinked in his pocket as if it had been a fortune in a handful of silver. Rye, and Ellen Terry waving a welcome from her garden above the old Tower! Rye, and his own garden, his own hushed, immemorial, red-walled garden, and the chimes sweetly sounding amid the purple shadows! And the grass-grown cobbles in the quiet little streets, and his rambles on the downs, his walks across the wind-swept marshes! His garden . . . how he had longed for it, for the budding pears and the opening tulips, for the still, soft summer mornings, and the break of day, and the pleasant sunny outlook over the lawn, the lawn all haunted with starlings and chaffinches—yes, even for the enfolding sea-fog, for the muffling snow of winter nights when the loud tick of the clock was the only sound. It was *his* anchorage, *his* little downward bur-row, his corner of the Europe that he had gone forth to conquer. Lamb House . . . one adorable touch at least of the tone of time.

An absorbing figure, an immortal symbol. For is he not the embodiment, complete and unparalleled, of that deep, that impossible yearning of which Hawthorne somewhere speaks—the yearning of the American in the Old World, "of the blood within his veins, for that from which it has been estranged, the half-fanciful regret that he should ever have been separated from these woods, these fields, these natural features of scenery, to which his nature was moulded, from the men who are still so like himself, from these habits of life and thought (though he may not have known them for two centuries) he still perceives to have remained in some mysterious way latent in the depths of his character, and soon to be reassumed, not as a foreigner would do it, but like habits native to him, and only suspended for a season"?

Towards the end of his life he planned a great pic-turesque book about London. He "put me," says Mr.

Gosse, "under gratified contribution by coming frequently to the House of Lords in quest of 'local color,' and I took him through the corridors and up into garrets of the Palace where never foreign foot had stepped before. There was not, to make a clean breast of it, much 'local color' to be wrung out, but Henry James was indefatigable in curiosity. What really did thrill him was to stand looking down from one of the windows of the Library on the Terrace, crowded with its motley afternoon crew of Members of both Houses and their guests of both sexes."

What thoughts, what memories trooped through his mind as he stood there, his face still pressed against the window of the earthly paradise? Did he recall those old English picture-books, wrapped in a golden haze, of which he had never ceased to turn the pages? Master Jacky, home from Eton for his Christmas holidays, and the charming young sisters with their pretty blue sashes, and the holly and the mistletoe and the gallant fox-hunting gentlemen? And *Mrs. Perkins's Ball* and Nash's *Mansions of England in the Olden Time?* And Thackeray's Boulogne, and the castles and the ruins, and all those old voices and graces of the past? And the Prince Imperial borne aloft, and that prodigious English family at Geneva who had irradiated such a strange historic light . . . yes, and the pouting young Marquise who had exhaled from afar the scented air of the Tuileries? The child had been father of the man; the man had never outgrown the child. And Europe had been a fairy-tale to the end.